JEFFREY D. WILHELM

Improving Comprehension
WITH
Think-Aloud Strategies

Modeling What Good Readers Do

■SCHOLASTIC

NEW YORK • TORONTO • LONDON • AUCKLAND • SYDNEY
MEXICO CITY • NEW DELHI • HONG KONG • BUENOS AIRES

Dedication

To all of the teachers with whom I have worked and learned,
especially the Boise State Writing Project teachers, and among
them especially Andrew Porter, Sarah Veigel, Rachel Bear, Debra
Smith, Erika Boas, and others too numerous to mention.

And to all of you who are dedicated to the art of teaching
because you love your students as learners.

Cover and Interior Designer: Maria Lilja
Copy/Production Editor: Danny Miller
Cover photo by Maria Lilja
Interior photos on page 7 by Jane Buchbinder; on pages 26, 51, 84, 110, 121, 132, and 135 by Wendy Murray; pages 64, 93, 158, and 163 by Michael C. York; and on page 150 by Vicki Kasala.

Scholastic has made every effort to identify the correct source for work in this book. Any work not correctly attributed will be attributed in future editions of this book.

ISBN: 978-0-545-21883-2

1 2 3 4 5 6 7 8 9 10   23   19 18 17 16 15 14 13 12

Contents

Acknowledgments

In college I had a Bible professor who wrote thank-you notes each November to people to whom he was grateful. He recommended it as a profoundly salutary and humbling pursuit. You could write a letter a day and never run out of folks to whom you feel grateful, he told me. He also said that almost everyone on your list, if not everyone, would be someone who had been your teacher. He meant both the teachers we have in schools and the teachers we meet throughout our lives: those who teach us by example, who lend us a hand when we need it, who mentor us through friendship and loving-kindness.

I've engaged in this project a few times, and my professor was right: Everyone I wrote to was and often continues to be a teacher to me. The process makes me feel connected to the world in a way I don't always feel. I realize that there are many people who have contributed to my development, encouraging me and helping me refine my thinking and my skills in varied pursuits, from teaching and research to cooking, kayaking, carpentry, and raising a family. It's humbling to engage in a project such as writing a book and to realize how many people have contributed, and recognize that I can't thank them all without filling up many more pages than are reasonably allowed for acknowledgments. It's also humbling to write a second edition and to realize how much you have learned in the meantime, often from those people who were supposedly your students. So let me begin by expressing gratitude to my teachers, and among them my students who have taught me so much.

First, my wife, Peggy Jo, and my daughters, Fiona Luray and Jasmine Marie, and my father, Jack Wilhelm. I need always to thank my friend and mentor Michael Smith for his constant guidance and patience. I thank George Hillocks and Bruce Novak for all they have taught me about teaching. I'd like to send off a 25 gun salute to all the teachers with whom I've worked through the Boise State Writing Project, particularly those teachers who were involved in our year long Advanced Reading Institute where we experimented bravely with think-alouds and made the DVD that accompanies this volume.

Thanks, of course, to my editors, Lois Bridges and Danny Miller, who helped to create and shape this project with their insightful editing and care. A grateful shout-out goes to Rachel Bear, with whom I have worked closely as a colleague, co-teacher, and CCSS implementer. Her help on this second edition was invaluable. And to Erika Boas for her help on this book and for very helpful ongoing conversations about reflective teaching and responding to student needs with new techniques and teaching implementations.

And again, I'd like to thank everyone who is a teacher. Without you, well, there would be no learning! I am eager to continue learning from you. If you use ideas in these books, adapt or elaborate on them in particular ways that you find successful, I'd be most gratified to hear and learn from you. I can be reached by e-mail at jwilhelm@boisestate.edu

Author's Note: Think-Aloud Strategies and the Common Core State Standards

In my opinion, the Common Core State Standards (CCSS) offer the best opportunity for progressive educational change that I have seen in more than 30 years as an educator. Using think-aloud strategies to promote more proficient reading, composing, and learning across topics, themes, and genres has never been more important. The CCSS represent a welcome and profound paradigm shift towards instruction that focuses on student expertise and the strategic tools that they need to excel across the disciplines.

Please note that these standards cannot be addressed, much less met, through business as usual. The standards call on every teacher to transform his or her teaching into a problem-oriented, meaning-making pursuit that develops effective strategic capacities. A robust body of research shows that developing strategic knowledge requires modeling, mentoring, and monitoring students' use of strategies in meaningful contexts—and how to do so is a major theme of the first few chapters of this book.

Look at the language of the CCSS: the standards use active production verbs such as *write*, *produce*, *research*, *argue*, and *persuade*. The later chapters of this book include engaging ideas for collaborative inquiry projects, opportunities for students to use technology and multimedia, and ways that you can draw on both formative and summative assessment to monitor and track your students' progress with Common Core and more (watch for the CCSS icons in the margins signaling a direct link). The comprehension and composition strategies I introduce in this book are useful in helping students to succeed as proficient, independent readers and composers of high quality, complex text.

Embracing the standards doesn't mean abandoning our smart, principled approach to informed teaching. What we know about time-tested research, best practices, and, particularly, those specific human beings who are our own students remains as critical as ever. Did you know that in a typical fourth-grade classroom, you're likely to find a reading span of seven grades—from a second-grade reading level all the way to ninth grade ability (Hargis, 2006)? Clearly, one size does not fit all. It makes sense, then, to provide our students with as many possible ways to access, comprehend, and converse with challenging texts of all kinds. Our struggling readers and writers, Limited Formal Schooling (LFS) students, and English Language Learners will succeed to the extent that we scaffold and differentiate our instruction.

Finally, the Common Core State Standards call for making our classrooms arenas of productivity and creativity (instead of consumption) where students may produce written work across genres, dramatic and theatrical performances, and create a wide range of artifacts from videos to museum exhibits. We need to move from places where kids only consume other people's meanings to places where they create their own.

This book will help you develop a productive repertoire of diverse teaching and learning strategies; what's more, you'll learn what contexts and strategies work best to assist students in becoming proficient readers and composers. Above all, you will promote a dynamic mindset (Dweck, 2009) of growth and potential in both your students and yourself that will lead to a lifetime of productive learning.

—Jeff Wilhelm
Boise, Idaho, July 2012

Introduction

This book originally appeared in 2001 as the first in a series of books I wrote for Scholastic about specific techniques for teaching students the process of reading and composing. The books—which also include *Action Strategies for Deepening Comprehension* (2002) and *Reading Is Seeing* (2004)— have been so successful that I have updated them all as second editions and have included accompanying DVDs that show teachers and students making use of various iterations of these techniques.

The premise behind these books is simple: the most important thing we can teach our students is how to learn. Or put another way, the most powerful thing we can provide to our students is *strategic knowledge*, a knowledge of the procedures people use to learn, to think, to read, to communicate, and to compose. The most effective way to introduce students to these tools is to model them in the contexts of meaningful tasks and then to assist students in their own use of these strategies through an ongoing process of supportive mentoring and monitoring.

For our purposes, this means that to help our students become expert readers, we must model the strategies of expert readers using authentic texts including comics, YouTube videos, novels, short stories, nonfiction books, newspaper articles, arguments, and Internet sites and then support students in taking on these expert strategies for themselves as they read independently.

Though this idea may seem obvious, it stands in direct contrast to the theories and practices that dominate most of American curriculum, instruction, and testing. Reviews of American education show that we spend most of our time teaching students information, filling them with declarative knowledge (the what) instead of assisting them to enact new and more proficient ways of reading, problem solving, and making meaning (the how).

This is unfortunate. As the research clearly shows, when students are asked to learn information without actively using procedures to construct understanding, they usually end up forgetting the what (the content). Never having learned the how, they are put squarely behind the eight ball and do not know how to learn on their own.

Several recent reviews have also shown that information-driven teaching can be boring and disengaging for many students. Students feel talked at and fail to get involved either emotionally or cognitively in the procedures of learning and making meaning.

In the 10 years since the first edition of this book appeared, I've continued to work, almost daily it seems, with think-alouds in my own teaching—with students from upper elementary to university graduate students. I can't imagine teaching without "thinking aloud," that process of making one's reading, thinking, or problem-solving processes visible and available to oneself and others by speaking, writing, or creating visuals of the process. Thinking aloud seems to come up in nearly every lesson, whether I've planned to use it or not. I've also worked to help interns and practicing teachers use the technique in all subject areas, with many different genres and data sets, with all kinds of kids (English Language Learners, limited formal schooling/refugee students, struggling readers, AP English—the gamut!). And finally, I've used think-aloud strategies very productively in several books and research studies, some of which have won awards (e.g., *Reading Don't Fix No Chevys* for my studies of boys and literacy).

This second edition includes new sections on how to teach with think-alouds and what can be taught with them. I've found that thinking aloud is a great way to model, mentor, and monitor students' strategic development with *any* kind of strategy from decoding words to interpreting symbols, to understand and use any kind of convention, and to read or write any kind of genre

Protocol a model template for navigating a procedure or task.

Think-alouds are a kind of "in-the-midst of the doing of it" report a protocol that highlights how one is navigating a task or reading as it is being done; i.e., the reporting out of what one is noticing, thinking, and doing as one reads a text or engages in another kind of problem-solving procedure.

with all the special conventions that each genre entails. I've also found that the technique can work at all levels of inquiry: as a way of inquiring into HOW we read most successfully, and as a way of comprehending WHAT we read as we build our conceptual understandings. Think-alouds are a way of reflecting on WHY, HOW, and WHAT we read—developing metacognitive awareness of our reading and problem-solving processes so that we have more control over them.

Thinking aloud can also help students practice and master, *in real reading contexts*, all the general processes of reading (activating background knowledge, decoding, visualizing/experiencing text, predicting, summarizing, questioning). Among many other benefits, teacher think-alouds provide models and "protocols" of how to approach different kinds of genres and deal with different textual conventions. As they do so, think-alouds:

- Create a safe way for all students to enter into text and be successful as readers and metacognitive beings, even with challenging texts and with new conventions like those for symbolism and understanding unreliable narrators.

- Focus students' attention on specific aspects and conventions of a text or phenomenon and help them see what they are being asked to do as a readers by these textual codes and cues.

- Foster and support higher-level, inquiry-based questioning and speculation.

- Encourage students to see patterns within texts and make connections to related texts or phenomena.

- Work toward understandings that can be used in future readings and in similar interpretive situations in life.

- Help students construct their own responses and achieve their own insights, for example, coming up with their own thematic interpretations including textual support or evidence identified during the think-alouds.

The second edition focuses on how think-alouds are a set of methods for inquiry-oriented teaching that fosters new ways of understanding in a context of inquiry. I'll show how all inquiry strategies are reading strategies, and how all reading strategies, when used robustly, are inquiry strategies.

We will also explore how think-alouds can be used as formative and summative assessments as a way for students to document their learning, and for teachers to do teacher research. I've found that student think-alouds are a great way to involve our students in self-assessment that helps them name and celebrate what they know and can already do while helping them figure out where to go next. The think-aloud technique is helpful to me as a teacher-researcher as I plan my own lessons and review the success (or relative success!) of my teaching. It helps me explore, with data from my students, how and why my teaching works and how it could work better. In this way, the technique helps both me and my students work toward "conscious competence," i.e., an understanding of what we know, how we know it, how we might do even better in the future.

This second edition will also explore the work I've been doing on using think-alouds with technological applications and different modalities, like doing an individual or group think-aloud with Googledocs, or creating PowerPoint process analyses. We'll also examine how to use think-alouds to respond to electronic and multimodal texts such as films, websites, paintings, and the like.

Accompanying DVD

Readers of the first edition (and there were lots of them—sales and resale figures indicate there may be nearly a quarter million of you!) often e-mailed me to ask for classroom modeling of various uses of the think-aloud technique. I am very pleased that this second edition is being released with a DVD, filmed during a "Camp Reading Rocks" sponsored by the National Writing Project. Many of the children featured on the DVD are ELL, LFS, or struggling readers. You will see a range of real teachers using thinking aloud for the first time with real kids. The DVD will show you how you can reasonably introduce the technique with your students to various ends. Where you will take the technique next is anybody's guess—the technique is so powerful and flexible that the stratosphere is the limit! For your convenience, the text in the following chapters is coded with icons referring you to particular examples from the DVD. Also on the DVD, look for tips and techniques and actual think-alouds from math, science, social studies, specials, and other content areas.

For your convenience, the text in the following chapters is coded with icons referring you to particular examples from the DVD.

If you'd like to see more video clips of me explaining a range of comprehension strategies and learning theory, check out the Curriculum Services of Canada (CSC): http://curriculum.org/content/about-csc. Type "Jeff Wilhelm" into the search line and a complete offering of my archived webcasts will pop up; it's all free—download and enjoy.

The Common Core State Standards

Finally, and perhaps most importantly, this second edition responds to the needs and requirements of current trends in educational policy, particularly those articulated by the Common Core State Standards (CCSS) which at this printing look to be adopted by the great majority of states, and which will certainly have an effect on all teachers across the country. The CCSS literacy standards are very friendly to inquiry approaches and focus throughout the grades on student activity (procedural/strategic knowledge), particularly in areas like ascertaining key details, inferencing, summarizing, determining and justifying main ideas, knowledge of genre and text structures, understanding multimodal features of texts, taking on relationships with authors, critiquing and evaluating text, and many more interpretive operations which are focused on specifically in this text. Most of the standards for reading and many for writing, such as writing arguments and providing evidentiary reasoning, are directly addressed here in ways that fit both the letter and the spirit of the new Common Core standards, as well as the next generation of assessments like the Smarter Balance and The Partnership for Assessment of Readiness for College and Careers (PARCC).

CHAPTER I

FREQUENTLY-ASKED QUESTIONS ABOUT THINK-ALOUDS

Over the years, in my think-aloud workshops and in e-mail exchanges with teachers around the world, I've collected a list of recurring questions about the think-aloud. Here are the most popular questions—with answers, too, of course!

What are think-alouds exactly?

In general, thinking aloud is a powerful way of modeling what experts do when they read, write, or solve problems by metaphorically "taking off the top of your head" and exhibiting what you are thinking, noticing, feeling, and doing while reading, etc. Thinking aloud makes invisible processes visible to students. One of the many great things about think-alouds is that students learn strategies *in context*—they learn while immersed in real units and inquiry projects, as they read real texts, and in this way, they can practice and eventually apply the strategies independently.

There are different kinds of think-alouds. The primary one for you is the **teacher/expert model** in which you name what you do, show and explain how you do it, explain why you do it, when you do it (naming the cues and tip-offs you respond to in the text), and how you monitor and self-correct while doing it. You do this, for example, to visibly demonstrate how to read, be it a reading where you are orchestrating general-process strategies or where you are focusing on how to read a particular genre like a lyric poem or lab report or complete a particular task like reading irony.

Free response think-alouds are when the reader reports out on whatever she is doing as she reads, without editing. I use these particularly at the beginning of a school year and at the end. I usually have my students name and code what they've done so I can easily see what they do as readers and how they think about it. This is great early in the school year to help students to self-assess, to engage them in tracing their growth throughout the school year, to provide discussion starters, and to help me as the teacher learn what individuals and groups of students already know and what they need to know. This helps me plan instruction, grouping, and so on.

Cued think-alouds are much more powerful instructionally because you are focusing on particular moves and interpretive strategies you want students to learn and are actively helping the kids use that strategy in context. This kind of think-aloud can be used to teach any kind of convention, strategy, or genre. Once the teacher models, she then underlines the kinds of cues being taught in a future reading for students to respond to. Eventually students notice the cues and respond to them in groups, pairs, and on their own.

How do think-alouds differ from "protocols"?

The term "think-alouds" is often used synonymously with "protocols" since "protocols" are a model for doing something, and an effective teacher think-aloud also provides such a model. When kids do and share think-alouds, they can come up with a "protocol" or "heuristic" together. They can develop a flexible, transportable thinking tool and a problem-solving repertoire that they can transfer to new situations. In this book I share a couple of these that my students and I have come up with together. My students put these "heuristics" or "protocols" on anchor charts or in flow charts showing, for example, the various ways you can go through the process of reading for symbols or reading an argument.

Anchor Standards for Reading, 1–10

What good are think-alouds? What can you teach with them?

Think-alouds can be used to model and assist students through reading anything, or thinking through any difficult problems or tasks. They talk and think their way through the task, and in turn, this "social speech" becomes "inner speech" that is unconsciously used to navigate tasks. If a task becomes difficult, we can review the think-aloud. For instance, if you drive an automatic five-speed and I throw you the keys to my Honda Insight, you'll just drive off—your inner speech about how to drive suffices. But if I throw you the keys to my tractor, you will have to think-aloud to navigate the task. "Put the key in the ignition... turn it slowly while depressing the first clutch..." Think-alouds can provide **explicit instruction** for any difficult strategy or process in the context of its actual use because in think-alouds, you explain and model

- *what a* strategy consists of.
- *why* a strategy is useful.
- *how* to perform the strategy in actual contexts of use.
- *when* to use the strategy in actual reading/problem-solving.
- guided practice and gradual release: teacher models, then teachers and students work together, then students working through iterations of the strategy with real text in the context of real inquiries.
- independent practice, students using the strategy on their own in reading, problem-solving and culminating projects.

(cf. Taylor, Harris, Pearson and Garcia, 1995)

Don't think-alouds interrupt the reading process?

Yes, but there are huge payoffs—all readers who use them develop deeper metacognitive awareness. Through think-alouds we can all share HOW we read as well as WHAT we read. This leads to improving our strategic facility and deepening textual understanding. Plus, good readers interrupt their own reading to stop, reflect, and make connections, so this is not unlike real expert reading. Think-alouds show kids what experts do—formalizing and placeholding.

Q&A 3: What do you do if students say "this is boring" or just shut down when you ask them to think out loud?

Don't the better readers get bored?

I do short excerpts that are challenging (what cognitive scientists call concentrated samples), and I only do think-alouds when there is a pay-off for everyone and when everyone can use them to meet an appropriate challenge. I really emphasize metacognitive awareness and control and how we can all grow and improve.

I also emphasize that we are a democratic community in the classroom, and that means that we all can get help when we need it. If you are good at a particular think-aloud or strategy, you can use it as an opportunity to help others. Most of the time you get to read on your own, but every now and then we do think-alouds which is an opportunity to be helped and to give help. I find kids really buy into this philosophy.

Teaching
Perspectives

When would you use think-alouds? How often?

On the one hand, I use think-alouds almost every day. I use short versions when I read aloud to students, and I use them whenever a student is having difficulty by saying, "let's think this through. What do we need to do? How do we know that?" On the other hand, I use formal think-aloud lessons only at the point of need, probably two or three times a unit when we are faced with a difficult text that requires strategies students are unfamiliar with or haven't yet mastered. I certainly don't do them just to do them; I use them strategically when students need them.

Q&A 2: How do
think-alouds help
less experienced
readers improve
comprehension?

How do you use them?

I love my six M's teaching model: Motivate, Model, Mentor, Monitor, and use Multiple Modalities and Measures. In other words, if there is something new to learn, I model a think-aloud showing how I address this kind of problem and how I use the appropriate strategy. I mentor by having students help me with a think-aloud, then I have them work together while I help them. Then they work together and alone as I monitor their progress, intervening as necessary. I also have students use variants like visual think-alouds. I like students to code their think-alouds to name what they are doing. In that way, I get in the multiple modalities and measures, or different ways of showing growth and achievement that are more powerful than grades.

How do you choose a think-aloud text or excerpt?

First, I use excerpts or texts from what we are already reading. In order to properly showcase the power of the think-aloud, these excerpts need to be challenging, rich, and important. If I am teaching a new strategy, then I'm going to look for what cognitive scientists call a "concentrated sample"—where we can really get a lot of practice on character cues or symbols in a short passage. I might also choose an excerpt from an important point in the text—the beginning, climax, ending, etc. I often use short texts from newspapers, the Internet, cartoons, or paintings, etc., that will help us practice the strategy being learned. It is very important that the text pertains to the unit so we are learning concepts and procedures together. I like to have students find interesting texts they can use to model a think-aloud or share with the class for a group think-aloud. You have to be sure to practice your teacher think-aloud models and keep working on them. Make sure that you are able to model and name what you are doing as a reader, and explain what you do to apply the strategy.

I'm sold, but how can I convince and help colleagues to use think-alouds and other reflective/metacognitive strategies?

Teachers need exactly what students need—purposeful and meaningful work, situated practice, assistance over time, and a clear vision of what they are doing and why they are doing it. They also need to understand how this project fits and works toward achieving what they value most. When you study WHAT you are learning, you tend to forget everything. When you focus on the HOW (which is what thinking-aloud does) you learn and retain the WHAT because you can't read without reading something; you can't think historically without knowing some history, etc. The only obstacle I've encountered is an information-driven approach to teaching—teachers who think their job is only teaching the WHAT, purveying information without teaching kids HOW to think like an expert reader, scientist, historian, and so on. If teachers can think of their job as apprenticing kids into new ways of thinking, knowing, and being in the world, which includes all the WHAT they are already teaching as well as the HOW, then they will embrace think-alouds as a great way to induct kids into more expert procedural knowledge. I've got some great activities in my book *Strategic Reading* (Wilhelm, et al, 2001) for thinking about this issue and moving people theoretically to a more learning centered and strategic approach.

Please note that the Common Core State Standards and the next generation of standards and assessments, not only in the U.S. but internationally, focus on *strategies* of learning—on the HOW versus the WHAT.

How do you persuade kids to use think-alouds?

It's not hard. Kids want to be active and they want to be competent; they want to learn how to think like an expert. In my studies on boys and literacy (Smith and Wilhelm, 2002; 2006), I found that kids give up when they have nothing meaningful to do or when they think they can't do something and they know they aren't going to get the help that they need. If the competence being developed is assisted through techniques like think-alouds, and if the competence is in service of knowing and doing something important (e.g., working towards understanding and completing culminating projects in inquiry contexts) then, in my experience, even very reluctant students can be brought to the point where they excitedly embrace thinking aloud and learning new material. You always have to emphasize to yourself and students: why are we doing this? what is it in service of? The think-aloud isn't important in itself, its importance lies in its service to comprehension and more competent reading.

What about standardized tests and kids' achievement?

When kids learn how to comprehend, monitor comprehension, solve problems, and think about their thinking and reading in flexible ways, they do better on the tests. There's a huge amount of research that shows this (see *Engaging Readers and Writers with Inquiry* for a full discussion). So even if you are under pressure for kids to perform well on standardized tests, think-alouds will help achieve that and so much more because they will be learning to read (and write and problem-solve) more and more like a real expert. Plus, the next generation of tests for the CCSS require strategic reading, writing, problem-solving, and metacognition. Think-alouds will help kids on these assessments.

What support do you need to teach with think-alouds?

This book is a great support. So is the DVD which provides models of real teachers trying out techniques that you can emulate and adapt. Like the Nike commercials, I'd say: *Just do it* and learn from doing it, making adjustments and improvements every time you use one. It is helpful to work together with peer teachers and coaches. Consider enlisting your students in finding think-aloud texts, modeling them to each other, and getting them to suggest ways the think-alouds work and ways that it could help more. But the real key is to try them and keep trying them. There's a huge amount of research that shows teachers improve by trying new things, and then sticking with those new techniques to improve them. Trying something once isn't really trying it. Trying something unreflectively isn't really trying it. When teachers try new techniques and reflect upon their use, it's been shown that their theories and other practices begin to evolve in powerful ways.

What about assessing think-alouds?

I think it's unethical to grade students on something you haven't taught them to do. I regard most think-alouds as practice in using a new, sophisticated strategy and in dealing with new and difficult concepts. Recent research in cognition has shown how important repeated practice is with different texts and in different situations as a way to consolidate and master skills. So I grade most think-alouds my students do on completion, on effort, and on improvement. They are great formative assessments but these really shouldn't be graded on quality, since the kids are in the process of learning. However, I have begun to use some think-alouds, and particularly a variation called the "process analysis," as a summative assessment—but only after students have had plenty of practice using the technique with particular strategies.

A process analysis requires metacognition and deep knowledge of problem-solving procedures. It tells the story of what students did and how they did it while reading a section of text, or while composing something or solving a problem, and is often more revealing and useful to me as a teacher than the actual composition or problem that was solved. The process analysis tracks understanding, allows me to see the student's process, and informs my teaching—showing me what I should reinforce, correct, or add in my upcoming teaching.

The Thinking Behind Think-Alouds: Vygotsky's Multi-Sided Model of Teaching and Learning

The teaching/learning theories of noted Russian psychologist Lev Vygotsky and his followers inform many of the ideas you will encounter in this book and the others in this series that show how action strategies, visuals, questioning, group structures, discussion, reading manipulatives, and critical lenses work as tools to help students consolidate and then outgrow their current capacities. Vygotsky's theories have been hugely influential on successful early-literacy programs like Reading Recovery® and Guided Reading, and his ideas are just beginning to gain a foothold in instruction for older students.

Vygotsky and neo-Vygotskians build their ideas on the premise that *what is learned must be taught.* Sounds simple enough, but as you will see when you read about the three basic models of teaching and learning today, most schools and much classroom activity runs counter to this notion and fails to fully understand what it means to teach. This, in my opinion, is the central reason for the shortcomings of American education—we have underappreciated and underarticulated what is actually required to teach, and therefore to learn.

The most prevalent teaching/learning model today is the *teacher/information-centered model,* in which teaching is the purveying of information (this model transforms the old saw "those who can't do, teach," to "those who can tell, teach"). This is considered a one-sided model because learning is centered on the information possessed by the teacher, which flows one way, from the teacher to the student.

A reaction against this model is the progressive *student-centered model,* in which the student independently pursues an interest of his choice. The teacher provides a nurturing environment for student exploration and discovery. This is also considered a one-sided model because learning is driven by the student (i.e., "those who can get kids to articulate and pursue their own interests, teach").

The third is a multi-sided *learning-centered model* in which expertise is given over to students in an exchange ("those who can do something, understand how to do that something, and can assist others to do it over time, teach"). This model stands in direct contrast to the prevailing one-sided teacher-centered, information-centered model. In the learning-centered model, the teacher teaches through the relationship cultivated with a student in the context of working together closely on a compelling problem of interest to them both and of interest in disciplinary study. It also goes well beyond the one-sided student-centered model in which students construct their own understandings in a nurturing environment but without the direct interventions of the teacher. In the learning-centered model, expertise is explicitly and continuously shared and collaboratively developed with the student, as teacher and student (and student with other students) engage together in purposeful, situated, meaningful, and productive shared activities.

I've always questioned the teacher-centered model because it focuses on what but not how. Research in cognitive science has made it compellingly clear that just telling students information is a weak form of teaching. Though the student-centered model is a major improvement over the teacher-centered model, I critique it as well because this model assumes that much learning occurs naturally. Given the conventionality of texts (i.e., given that texts are constructed in certain ways not because of nature but because people have agreed to construct and read them in certain ways), I do not believe that we learn to read naturally. A child locked in a room with books would not learn to read them on her own; she needs someone to teach her how print works and what she is expected to do as a reader. I would also argue that the teacher who believes in natural learning often deprives the student of her full expertise as a reader. Even something so simple as directionality in reading is entirely conventional; we read left to right but some cultures read right to left (Korean) or up and down (Hebrew). Reading and composing are based on cultural agreements. Therefore, students must be inducted into these agreements—they are not natural, but cultural.

And so I champion the multi-sided learning-centered model based on Vygotsky: learning is the crucial element, and we recognize that teaching and learning are two sides of the same coin, two parts in the same dance, but with multiple dimensions of why, how, what, when, and where all informing the teaching and learning. (For a fuller discussion, see Wilhelm, et al, 2001.)

The Vygotskian View of Reading

According to Vygotsky and his followers, we must learn ways of reading and thinking in order to participate fully in our culture and to make meaning within it; these ways have to be passed from experts to novices in the context of meaningful, collaborative activity. For them, a book is more than just words on a page or a narrative that will move us or inform us; it is a highly conventionalized form of language. Authors and readers use agreed-upon sets of conventions in order to convey meaning and make meaning, from knowing that quotation marks signal that a character is speaking to subtler codes signaling a character's intention or reliability. Teaching these conventions requires a more expert reader to notice what a novice reader currently understands (or misunderstands) and then to assist her to a higher level of understanding. This is *teaching* because it actively assists and promotes growth. Think-alouds are a powerful way to teach because they give students the expert's keys to unlock a text's fullest construction of meaning as well as a wide-awake understanding of how these conventions work so that procedural knowledge is developed and transferred to new reading and composing situations. Students are taught through this process to read like a writer, and to write like a reader.

Vygotsky's Zones

Vygotsky maintained that every child has a cognitive zone of actual development (ZAD). This zone is defined by what the child can do on her own without any kind of assistance. Vygotsky believed that if you give a child a task, like reading a book, and he does it, then you have taught him nothing. The child could already do the task, as that task was in his current zone of actual development. Further, Vygotsky argued that if you give a child a task to do and he cannot do it, then you have the chance to teach. If the child cannot do the task alone but can do it with a more expert person's help, then the task lies in what Vygotsky calls the zone of proximal development (ZPD). In this zone, students can do with help what they cannot do alone. Vygotsky argued that we can teach students something new only when the task is within their zone of proximal development.

What's the end goal? A classroom full of independent, engaged readers. You'll see an example of "teaching in the zone" in Chapter 1 (page 22) as I use a think-aloud to teach a student named Josh. Josh could identify and discuss the literal details of Walter Dean Myers' novel *Monster*, but he could not make the inferences needed to fully comprehend the text. Understanding the directly stated details was within his zone of actual development; making even simple inferences was within his zone of proximal development, meaning that he needed me to help him infer before he could do it on his own.

The think-aloud made the strategy of inferring tangible to Josh, putting the process in a concrete form that he could study, consider, respond to and appropriate for his own use. This process supports Vygotsky's assertion that all learning proceeds from the concrete to the abstract, and from the visible and external to the internal. In the chart that follows, I provide an overview of Vygotsky's model of learning.

Vygotskian Perspective: Teacher/Student Interactions

Student Responsibility ➡ **Teacher Responsibility** ➡ **Joint Responsibility** ➡ **Self Responsibility**

Zone of Actual Development	Zone of Proximal Development			New Zone of Actual Development
What the student can do on her own unassisted	Assistance provided by more capable others: teacher or peer or environment: classroom structures and activities	Transition from other assistance to self-assistance	Assistance provided by the self	Internalization, automatization

SOCIAL SPEECH

- Adult uses language to model process
- Adult and student share language and activity

PRIVATE SPEECH

- Student uses for herself language that adults use to regulate behavior (self-control)

INNER SPEECH

- The student's silent, abbreviated dialogue that she carries on with self that is the essence of conscious mental activity
- Private speech is internalized and transformed to inner verbal thought (self-regulation)

Adapted from Wilhelm, Baker, and Dube, 2001

The Zones

Vygotsky's concept of cognitive learning zones is so critical to appreciating this book—and to effective teaching—that I recap it here:

Zone of Actual Development—Independence: When we give a student a task in the zone of actual development, the student can already independently complete the task and there is nothing new to be learned, though such tasks may build confidence and fluency (some researchers believe that nearly half of school time is spent teaching things that most of the kids already know and can do). Reading inventories designate texts that students can comprehend on their own as being at the "independent" reading level. These are texts that students can comprehend on their own and therefore reading such texts is in that child's zone of actual development.

Within the Zone of Proximal Development—Instruction and Learning Occurs: If we give students a task within their zone of proximal development, the opportunity for learning is there, provided we give the proper support and assistance. With assistance (teaching), students can do things they could not do before. Learning will occur! We provide for support until we see that students can accomplish the task without help, until the skill has moved into their zone of actual development. Reading inventories designate texts that students can comprehend with expert assistance as being at the "instructional" reading level. At this level, students will be successful with instructional help. As students are provided with help to read texts at this level, they learn new strategies of reading and achieve understanding in how certain textual conventions and text structures work to make meaning. The child becomes a more expert and knowledgeable reader by being assisted through this zone.

Beyond the Zone of Proximal Development—Frustration: If we give students a task that is beyond the zone of proximal development, then it will be too hard no matter how much support we give (e.g., if we try to teach Shakespeare, with its alternating speakers, stage directions, and other special conventions, to students whose sight vocabulary is low and who have never read dramatic scripts, then they may not succeed with the text no matter how much help we provide). Reading inventories designate texts that a student cannot comprehend—even with assistance—as being at her frustrational reading level. These are texts that a student cannot comprehend and find frustrating; the text lies *beyond* the student's zone of proximal development.

Book Notes

For More on Vygotskian Teaching

Strategic Reading: Guiding Students to Lifelong Literacy (Wilhelm, Baker, and Dube, Heinemann/Boynton-Cook Publishers, 2001) further explores how Vygotsky's theory can be applied to the teaching of reading. It includes strategies such as front loading to teach strategies and activate background knowledge before reading, teaching questioning strategies for more critical reading, using inquiry projects and social-action projects to deepen students' reading, and many other strategies. It would make a perfect companion to this book.

Active Teaching in the ZPD: Offering Explanation, Modeling, Guided Practice

To teach in the zone of proximal development, Vygotsky says the teacher must first generously model how to work through a task, highlighting and naming how a particular strategy or strategies can be used to successfully complete it. Then the teacher needs to provide opportunities for students to try the strategy, with various levels of assistance. After modeling, a teacher then has students work in small groups, so they can assist one another, and so that she can circulate among them, helping when students get stuck. As the teacher notes evidence of students using the strategy effectively, she then provides a task in which students who are ready can use the strategy unassisted. If a student has trouble, the teacher can move him back a step by having him work with a peer or with the teacher herself. Ultimately, she looks for evidence that students can use the strategy completely on their own, applying it and adapting it to new learning tasks. For example, after teaching Josh the strategy of inferring using the novel *Monster*, (see page 30) I would watch to see that Josh used inferences when reading another novel, during a class discussion of an article on cloning in *Time for Kids*, or in his reading journal. In other words, I look to see that a student has internalized new strategic knowledge and uses it independently and automatically. I look to see that the new strategy is now within his ZAD.

This is the goal of all teaching and learning—independence.

Six Recursive Steps of Explicit Instruction

Remember, modeling doesn't stop after you've introduced a strategy. Throughout this teaching process, lend kids your strategic knowledge through active modeling and by stating what you are attending to. Literacy researchers Taylor, Harris, Pearson, and Garcia (1995) identify six recursive steps that occur in this kind of explicit instruction. When you read about Josh in the next chapter, you can refer to this list to see how I went through each of these steps.

1. Teacher explains what a strategy consists of.

2. Teacher explains why this strategy is important.

3. Teacher explains when to use the strategy in actual reading (e.g., what to notice in a text that tips off the reader that this particular strategy should be used).

4. Teacher models how to perform the strategy in an actual context (e.g., by doing a think-aloud using a real text) while students observe.

5. Teacher guides learner practice. Teachers and students work together through several increasingly challenging examples of the strategy using authentic texts. Teacher gradually releases responsibility to the students, allowing them to do what they are capable of on their own and intervening and supporting only when needed and only as much as is absolutely needed.

6. Students independently use the strategy as they pursue their own reading and projects.

Do As I Say—And As I Do!
The Steps of Passing Strategic Expertise to Students

Teacher Does/Students Watch
Step 1: Modeling of Strategy

- Teacher uses and talks about strategy through use of technique like think-alouds.
- Students observe.
- Teacher stresses what, why, and when of strategy use.

Teacher Does/Students Help
Step 2: Apprenticeship of Use

- Teacher uses strategy.
- Students help out identifying when and how strategy should be used.

Students Do Together/Teacher Helps
Step 3: Scaffolding Strategy Use

- Students use and talk about strategy with help of scaffolding technique like think-alouds, usually in small groups or pairs.
- Teacher observes, provides feedback, and helps as needed.

Students Do Alone/Teacher Watches
Step 4: Independent Use

- Student independently uses strategy, demonstrating competence through techniques like think-alouds
- Teacher observes and assesses; plans future instruction

Adapted from Wilhelm, Baker, and Dube, 2001

Vygotsky's take on learning is incredibly liberating. In his view, any child can learn the next more challenging strategy or concept if given supportive instruction. Children can and will learn, no matter the obstacles, if the learning is meaningful and they are given the right help at the point of need. If students are not progressing, Vygotsky would assert that the instruction has not been appropriate, thereby rejecting the view of Jean Piaget that the child may have plateaued in a particular developmental stage. George Hillocks' influential research (1995) uses classroom data to make the same case. He draws on Benjamin Bloom's (1976, 1985) research on human potential to argue that almost any child can and will learn given the right opportunities and instruction. This is a wonderful and powerful position for us to embrace; if we give our developing readers the right kinds of help, then they can and will learn to be better readers.

This book and the others in this series are dedicated to this end: to help provide you with flexible techniques for giving the right kind of help to your students, assistance that will move them through the steps of ***modeling, mentoring*** (apprenticeship, scaffolded use), and ***monitoring*** of independent use, so they can become confident, motivated, and engaged readers who can and will read throughout their lives.

The Place of Strategy Instruction in Your Reading Program

Anchor Standards for Reading, 1–10

In my previous books on teaching reading, I've maintained that reading well is a potentially life-transforming pursuit because it allows us to outgrow ourselves and become more than we currently are. This can only happen for our students if we fully embrace the idea that good reading requires good teaching, and that the more reluctant the readers we teach, the better and more powerful our teaching must be. But as we teach our students, there are several things to remember so that strategy instruction isn't overemphasized to the point that it interferes with, rather than supports, engaged reading.

- Reading strategies are important only insofar as they assist readers to construct meaningful understandings of authentic and compelling texts. With this level of comprehension, readers can respond to, converse with, and even resist the meanings the author seems to put forth.

- Teaching strategies are important only insofar as they assist readers to comprehend and respond to text. In other words, think-alouds are a useful teaching strategy when they help a reader through her zone of proximal development, helping her develop a particular strategy or set of strategies that she cannot yet use independently so she can engage with a text important to her current purposes.

- Think-alouds, like any teaching strategy, are not appropriate when students already know how to use a featured reading strategy, when they do not have a need to use the strategy, or when the strategy is so complex that it lies beyond their zone of proximal development. Once a new strategy is mastered, the scaffolding (provided by an instructional intervention like think-alouds) should be removed so students can use what they have learned independently to engage with the text.

The teaching and grouping structures explored throughout this book can provide various levels of support to whole-class, small groups, or individuals. They will help you with whole-group instruction but also with differentiating instruction to teach small groups or individuals in their zones of proximal development. The key is to use the strategy instruction flexibly. For example, if students have a general need to know a strategy in the context of a unit or reading, then I will teach them as a whole group. Often, because my students read with widely differing abilities, I will flexibly group them for strategy instruction. When I have the time, I find it most effective to work with students one-on-one. This is particularly important when a student has a unique need or when others in the class have already learned the strategy. If you use a workshop approach or have inquiry stations in your classroom, such tutoring can easily take place within these structures.

Sometimes I use more able readers to tutor less able ones. I find that even able readers benefit hugely from using think-alouds (both in the role of student and more expert peer) to name and consolidate their own current strategy use and to find ways of extending and elaborating on that use.

The bottom line: think-alouds are a means to an end—and that end is engaged and reflective reading. Use the technique flexibly to hand reading power over to your students. I've found that I use variations on thinking aloud nearly every day in my teaching, usually to provide very short models of my own reading and thinking processes, and other times in more sustained ways to provide rich models *for* student learning, or mentoring and monitoring *as* and *of* student learning. But always, the thinking aloud is purposeful and focused like a laser on student activity and on learning how to read, compose, and problem-solve more and more like a real expert.

CHAPTER 2

SEEING READING AS INQUIRY

Making Strategic Knowledge Visible and Available to Students

As I write this second edition, I've just returned from a kayaking trip down Idaho's Main Salmon—the so-called "River of No Return"— with my daughter Jasmine, now 18 years old and soon to be off to college. Just prior to descending Salmon Falls—one of the tougher drops on the river—we did a think aloud about how to roll our kayaks "into" a wave, a difficult maneuver sometimes necessary on this tricky stretch of river. In fact, we both had to execute this move on our way down, myself at the top of the rapids and Jasmine at the bottom. At the end of the run, we high-fived and talked about our little adventure, and how glad we were to have rehearsed our strategies and possible moves with a "think-aloud." The collaborative think-aloud helped us both "pre-set," "feedforward," (vs. feedback) and be prepared to put

CCSS

Anchor Standards
for Reading, 1–10

our strategies into immediate and independent action at the point of need. Less than a week later, I am reading the following section about her from the first edition of this book, when she was an 8-year-old, and I'm having a good laugh at how well think-alouds have aided us both over the last 10 years!

The Think-Aloud: Tracking Our Inner Voice

It was our first overnight whitewater canoe trip. My partner was my younger daughter, Jasmine, who at age 8 was already a "hammerhead," whitewater parlance for a gutsy and proficient canoeist. As we neared Little Falls on Maine's St. Croix River, we could hear the thunderous rumble of cascading rapids and see the water vapor rising from the horizon line of the river. These class III rapids would provide a real challenge to our abilities as a canoe team. We pulled over to the western bank so we could scout out possible routes. I asked Jasmine to tell me her plans for this canoe run. I needed to see if she understood how to successfully approach this new challenge and to have the opportunity to correct or help her if she did not. It was also important because we needed to agree on what to do so we could work together.

"Okay, Pappy," she started, taking a deep breath, "I think we should go river left." I followed her pointing finger. "And hit the "V" between those two big rocks. We'll be okay till we hit those pillow rocks down below. I'll give you a right draw and you sweep on the left to get around them. Hmmm… Once we get around that we need to hit that lower "V." I think we should eddy out behind the big rock and then peel out into the main current. Then it's easy and we have fun the rest of the way down!"

She looked at me to see what I thought.

"Mmmm. Good thinking," I agreed. "That strategy would work." Jasmine was using the language, commands, and strategies of canoeing to map out a good plan. By having her think-aloud, I was able to access and judge her ideas… and intervene in ways that might help.

"But that's pretty technical and there's not too much room for error. I think there is an easier way," I suggested.

"You mean over here on river right?"

"Yes," I nodded.

"It looks easy below, but what about the pillow rocks right here?" she asked, throwing a rock into the first drop of the river right below us where barely submerged rocks formed a wall all the way across the current.

"If we have enough momentum we'll make that drop to the right of this rock, punch over the wall of rocks, draw left around the big rock below, and then head to the main current and be golden. What do you think? What route would be best?"

A few moments later we were blasting down Little Falls river right, yelling to each other the commands we had already rehearsed during our think-aloud: "Left draw!"

"Right sweep!" and even an occasional "Yippee!"

The think-aloud had been a great rehearsal for successfully completing our challenge. We had so much fun—and both felt so competent—that Jasmine made me carry the canoe up the portage trail two times so we could put in more rapid runs!

I chose to describe a think-aloud from the "real world" to show that this talking-through of an endeavor is natural and a central way we help ourselves prepare and achieve—by saying aloud new steps until they become a part of our "inner voice" of automatized knowledge.

In the classroom, a think-aloud supports readers as they hit the sometimes-rough currents of the more difficult kinds of texts they begin to face in upper elementary and middle school. Just as my daughter Jasmine had to know the specific demands of that stretch of the St. Croix River to keep from capsizing, taking her cues from the shapes and positions of rocks, the eddies, and currents, a reader has to know the underlying conventions of a text in order to keep meaning "afloat." Without understanding what an author expects us to notice—whether it's a novelist's clue in dialogue about a character's deceit or a scientist's textbook bar graph showing rising air pollution—comprehension cannot take place. Think-alouds allow all students to hear how others sleuth out and make sense of all these text clues so that they can recognize and adopt these strategies as their own.

See, Think, Wonder

The specific think-aloud technique I'd used with Jazzy is called a "See Think Wonder" and combines visualizing and thinking aloud. Jazzy had taken a close look at the river to "see" its features—she was, in fact, "reading" the river. She then interpreted what she saw, "thinking" aloud as it were to make her thinking and planning visible to herself and to me, and to rehearse future action. Finally, I offered a prompt to get her "wondering" about other possibilities, essentially asking her "what would happen if. . . ?" This put her in the position of an active meaning-maker and decision-maker, and put us both in an agentive narrative where our choices would make a difference to our lived-through experience of canoeing the river. I foregrounded reading the river and canoeing it as something we had control over through our noticing, interpreting, considering all alternatives, and eventual decision making. (For more on this technique, see the DVD and the visualization book in this series.)

Tracking the Trail of a Porpoise

Q&A 1: What is a think-aloud and how does it improve reading comprehension?

So, a think-aloud of reading is creating a record, either through writing or talking aloud, of the strategic decision-making and interpretive processes of going through a text, reporting everything the reader is aware of noticing, doing, seeing, feeling, asking, and understanding as she reads. A think-aloud involves talking about the reading strategies you are using and the content of the piece you are reading.

However, it's wise to keep in mind that the report will be partial. Jasmine's canoeing think-aloud certainly did not reveal all her thinking and feelings. Think-alouds are also inexact reproductions of a person's actual thinking about reading; no one can thoroughly and accurately capture all of what he sees in his mind's eye. For these reasons, a think-aloud has been described as allowing us "to track the trail of a porpoise" because it gives us glimpses into hidden activity, allowing us to infer what is happening below the surface of consciousness. This is an apt analogy, because reading well is a highly complex activity, and there's much about it we don't understand—and may never know. I think we teachers need to remind ourselves of that fact. Learning to read well is tough going. As my daughter Fiona said to me when she was beginning to read more challenging books on her own, "Reading can be fun, but it can also be very frustrating!"

What the Research Says

In their seminal text *Verbal Protocols of Reading*, Pressley and Afflerbach trace the use of think-alouds from the time of Aristotle and Plato as a way of revealing and studying processes of thinking. In the last century, think-alouds have been used to develop psychological theory, understand problem solving in physics, reveal student strategy use and improvement during particular instructional interventions on various challenges, and to explore multiple other processing tasks.

I learned about think-alouds from the research literature on reading, where this technique—usually referred to as *protocols*—has been very useful in opening a window to understanding the highly complex and largely invisible processes of readers, writers, scientists, and others at work. As Pressley and Afflerbach report, "The human achievement of reading has few if any equals." These authors also provide an overview of how protocol research has helped us to understand the incredible complexity of reading and how it might be taught, to diagnose reading difficulties, and to monitor student readers' strategy use. My own research (see, for example, Wilhelm, 1997; 2008, Smith and Wilhelm, 2002; 2006; 2010) has explored how think-aloud protocols can be used not only as a research technique but as a powerful way to instruct and assist students to understand and use more complex processes of reading.

In fact, my colleagues Tanya Baker and Julie Dube-Hackett and I found that a major reason students struggle as readers in late elementary and middle school is because teachers underestimate the difficulty of the texts they are asking their students to read, including sophisticated narratives and expository texts, and therefore fail to provide the necessary assistance to help them successfully read these texts (Wilhelm, Baker, and Dube-Hackett, 2001).

A Think-Aloud in Action: Helping Josh Infer

Anchor Standards
for Reading, I, 4, 5, 6

Here's an example of how think-alouds help me to assess and then assist a student who is having trouble. I was working with Josh, a lively sixth grader who, along with the rest of the class, was independently reading Walter Dean Myers' young-adult novel *Monster*. In this book, a young man named Steve Harmon is jailed for participating as an accomplice in a burglary that results in a murder. He keeps a diary of his experiences in prison and during the trial, alternating between regular diary entries and a screenplay script he is writing about his experiences. Though it is clear that Steve was asked to help with the burglary, it is unclear if he actually did so. There is great tension as Steve's prison experiences become more threatening and the trial winds to an uncertain conclusion. Josh liked the book because it is about a "boy like me" "who's in big trouble" and because some of "it's written like a movie."

Twice during our reading of the book, I had photocopied some pages onto half a sheet of paper and Josh had written a think-aloud, putting down what he was doing as a reader next to the text segments where he was doing it. From these think-alouds I knew that Josh was literally comprehending the story but he was not making any kinds of inferences about the facts he was reading. Like many struggling readers, he understood the literal text but not the implied subtext. He wasn't engaged in connecting the dots and seeing patterns of implied meaning that are the true power of literary meanings like themes.

When he completed the novel, he had this to say:

Josh: There's one big thing I don't get. Did Steve Harmon take part in the robbery [that led to the murder] or not? I mean, it's bogus that he [the author] doesn't even tell us!

This comment confirmed for me that Josh needed my help to make some simple inferences. This was a slightly more sophisticated text than he was used to reading and it required him to infer by filling in gaps, and by seeing both simple implied relationships between details fairly close to each other and more complex implied relationships connecting and interpreting ideas from throughout various parts of the text. I knew that using additional think-alouds could help him to do these things.

WHAT: First, I explained to Josh what he needed to do. I told him that expert readers go beyond the directly stated facts of a story and make inferences—they connect separate pieces of information, make guesses about missing scenes and data, and elaborate on story facts to make a more complete story. "You can answer your question about Steve by making some inferences. In fact, the author has laid out some clues for you and he expects you to pick up on these and make some inferences!"

WHY: I explained to Josh why the strategy was important. "Most stories don't tell the whole story. You have to fill in gaps and read between the lines. The author gives you point A and point E and you have to walk to points B, C and D. If you don't make inferences, then quite often, you won't really understand the story. Plus, it's more powerful and fun to figure things out then to be directly told—it's like the fun of solving a puzzle or figuring out a play to beat the other team."

WHEN: Josh and I talked about when inferring is important in life and in reading. I asked him how he could infer if I was in a good mood and why making such an inference might be important. We talked about times when he had only told someone part of a story and how the audience might infer the rest of what happened. I told Josh I would help him see where *Monster* invited him to make inferences: when there was a story gap, an unexplained connection, or an unanswered question. I asked, "Why do you sometimes leave certain things unsaid? Why might an author do this too?" Josh smiled, "Like when I don't want my mom to know what I really did, or when I want someone to figure something out for himself."

I then asked Josh when he most believed Steve. "When he writes in his journal," he quickly answered.

"Most excellent!" I replied. "You are a reading prodigy, I can see already!"

Josh gave me a half smile, indicating that he thought I was hallucinating and that he didn't know what the word prodigy meant.

HOW: I told Josh I would model how to infer as I thought aloud through my reading of the book's first few journal entries. In the first one, I got to this point in the diary entry. I read all the words of the story aloud and then inserted my thinking aloud as I did so (my thinking aloud is in bold).

Text	Think-Aloud
"You thinking about cutting a deal?" King asked.	Geez, why would King threaten him? They're both on trial. They should be in this together.
King curled his lip and narrowed his eyes.	Yes, he is definitely threatening Steve! He is making a face at him to let him know he better not be making a deal and finking on him. But why would Steve need to cut a deal? Why would King be worried about him cutting a deal?

LENDING EXPERTISE: I was careful not to answer Josh's driving question. My interest wasn't in answering his question but in helping him learn a new process of reading that would allow him to answer his question on his own *and* help him in the future. My role was to point out where to look for information that might answer his questions and to model what to do with it—that is, to use the information to infer what the author wants us to understand about a character. With *Monster*, Walter Dean Myers is too good a writer to explicitly tell us that King is threatening Steve or why; he instead invites us to "fill in the gap" and infer an answer. Much as the pointillist painter Georges Seurat carefully placed thousands of small dots of color on a canvas, expecting us to use our mind's eye to fill in the gaps—to blend them to see a sunlit day in a Paris park—novelists invite us into a delightful process of reenvisioning their details and co-constructing their story with them so that we can experience it fully and make it our own.

GUIDED PRACTICE: Later in the novel, I had Josh think aloud as he read a couple of diary entries, but I underlined key sections that required an inference. These underlines helped Josh become familiar with the kinds of moments in a text that signal a need for a reader to pose questions and infer. Kids need to know that authors are in a sense continually extending different invitations to the reader such as: come in, visualize this scene; caution, with these details about facial expressions and her tone of voice I'm telling you that she doesn't mean what she just said. I was providing Josh with guided practice in noticing and interpreting such invitations to make inferences before I set him on his own. Here's an example:

Text	Think-Aloud
Anybody can walk into a drugstore and look around. Is that what I'm on trial for? I didn't do nothing!	But Steve testified that he wasn't in the drugstore! So he was lying! Maybe he was trying to cover something up? But what would he be trying to cover up?
I thought about writing what happened in the drugstore, but I would rather not have it in my mind.	How could he write about it if he wasn't there? He must have been there! So he lied in the court. But why was he there? Did that mean he helped with the robbery? No wonder his lawyer doesn't believe him.

Inferring Is Crucial to Reading: Interpretive Strategies to Model for Kids

As I told Josh, quoting the great writer Umberto Eco, "Reading is the taking of inferential walks. The text offers point A and point E, and the reader must walk points B, C, and D to reach point E." Reading of all kinds requires continual inference-making, because so much of what an author communicates is not directly stated.

When working with a specific set of strategies, particularly complex ones such as inferring, I always find it useful to name for students the strategies we will use, the tip-offs in the text that remind us to use them, and how they will benefit us. Doing so makes very complex reading operations clearer and more accessible to students. It also "placeholds" the techniques and makes them more available as students go through their zone of proximal development to acquire and develop mastery. Following is an elaborated example of the kind of chart I devised with Josh and his classmates as we learned about inferring. (For more examples of guidance for using these kinds of "task-specific" reading processes, see Chapter 6).

SCAFFOLDING: After several short think-aloud episodes where I underlined cues that were meant to stimulate inferences, Josh said that he thought he understood what inferring meant, could recognize when he was invited by authors to make inferences, and he also thought he had "kind of" an answer to his question: Steve was in the drugstore because he was supposed to help with the robbery but that it was left unclear whether he actually did help. "I think the author left it unclear on purpose," Josh told me, "to make us more involved… we're just like the jury then, judging him and trying to figure it out, if he's a monster or not. Personally, I think he decided not to help with the robbery and he was definitely out of there when the murder happened."

I talked with Josh then about how his evaluation of Steve's character led him to this conclusion and how that made him feel about the end of the book. Given Josh's enthusiasm for this story, and his growing ability to make inferences, I recommended that he read John Marsden's *Letters from the Inside*. "It's a mind-blowing book and it requires some major league inferring. Think you are up for it?" I asked Josh. He responded by borrowing the book and giving me a high-five. We discussed his reading of that book over several occasions, though in much less structured ways then we had worked through *Monster*, and it was clear that Josh was truly getting the hang of how to make inferences.

Expert readers comprehend the literal text, make inferences based on textual details, and identify the clues upon which they have based their inferences by

- noticing and comprehending literal details and building on these to predict future action and elaborate on the textual world.
- noticing and filling textual gaps with relevant meaning.
- noticing, connecting, and interpreting simple implied relationships. (A reader must recognize a relationship that is not directly stated in the text. Readers must make an inference by connecting and interpreting a few pieces of information that occur close together in the text.)
- noticing, connecting, and interpreting complex implied relationships. (Readers must infer a relationship and see a pattern from a large number of details that occur in different places throughout a text. In order to answer such a question about a complex implied relationship a student must be able to "identify the necessary details, discern whatever patterns exist among them, and then draw the appropriate inference.") (Hillocks 1980, 308)

Expert readers do this so they can

- make valid inferences about characters and their relationships.
- make valid inferences about setting (the time and place).
- make valid inferences about past, present, and possible future action.
- infer and identify the text type and its expectations of the reader, i.e., recognize whether the text is nonfiction or fiction, realistic or fantasy, makes use of satire or irony, etc.
- infer and identify the mood and emotional tone of a text.
- identify the point of view and attitude toward the material presented.
- differentiate between the narrator and the author of a text.
- infer the narrator's attitude toward the subject, others in the text, and the reader.
- judge the narrator's reliability. (Should we believe the narrator, and to what degree?)
- infer the author's attitude toward the subject and toward the audience.
- use sets of inferences to figure out what an author is trying to communicate, i.e., the author's implicit meaning or "authorial generalization" about the subject matter.
- elaborate and extend the text, applying it to future situations that go beyond the text itself.

What Think-Alouds Can Do for Teachers: Opening the Window on Strategic Instruction

Our goal for students is engaged reading—that emotional and cognitive state when you are involved in a text to the fullest, using an author's words to get inside someone else's skin, understand another's point of view, connect this perspective to your own, converse with characters or an author, learn new information, and mysteriously come out with a changed understanding of yourself and your world.

Many of our students are not engaged readers and are not sure why the struggle to become one is worth it. More than that, they don't really know how to get started—they don't know what expert readers know and do when they read or how they might start doing these things too. It is our job to help them, and it's not a simple task. In fact, when I work with preservice and practicing teachers, I often start my coaching by telling them, "You have a big problem. Well, you have at least one big problem that I know about!" The problem is that they (like you) are expert readers, and as such, they are unaware of all the cognitive, emotional, and visual processes they enact as they read. So automatic is their expert reading that it's hard for them to grasp the difficulties of those who most need their help, those who are least like them, the kids who are unmotivated to read and who don't do it very well. This makes it hard for us expert readers to teach these kids who don't understand why someone should want to read, much less to set about doing it in more productive ways. Think-alouds can provide immeasurable help. They make us slow down and take a look at our own reading process. They show us what students are doing—and not doing—as they engage in the reading process, and they help students to take on our expert strategies by providing a means of modeling, mentoring, and monitoring more expert reading.

Think-Alouds Can Help Teachers to . . .

- deepen their own awareness of the reading process.
- use this heightened awareness of their strategic and interpretive processes to help model these strategies to kids.
- mentor students, individually or in groups, to take on the stances and strategies of expert readers.
- see what students do and don't do as they read, which helps the teacher to assess students and plan appropriate instruction in the students' zone of proximal development.

- understand what in a text confuses readers; assess students' use of strategies; diagnose and address specific problems.
- support readers to identify problems and monitor their own comprehension.
- monitor their independent use and assess students naturalistically, through real reading performances instead of with decontextualized questions or standardized measures.

Think-Alouds Can Be Used to Model...

- general processes of reading, like predicting, monitoring, and summarizing.
- task-specific processes like understanding symbolism, irony, or bar graphs.
- text-specific processes like understanding the structure of an argument and evaluating its effectiveness.

Ways to Present Think-Alouds

As you will see throughout this book, think-alouds can be introduced and used in a variety of ways, e.g., in spoken, written, or visual formats; on Post-it notes, overheads, butcher paper, or notebook paper; with or without technology.

Written think-alouds have the advantage of providing a record of reading activity that can be shared, manipulated, saved, assessed, compared to earlier and later efforts to gauge and demonstrate improvement, etc. These visible signs of accomplishment are very important to less able readers. They can be used to celebrate improvement, provide the assistance to meet reasonable goals, put in a portfolio to show actual proof of accomplishment and process, and so forth. Basic ways to conduct think-alouds are

- Teacher does think-aloud; students listen. (modeling)
- Teacher does think-aloud; students help out. (mentoring)
- Students do think-alouds as large group; teacher and other students monitor and help. (mentoring)
- Students do think-alouds in small group; teacher and other students monitor and help. (mentoring)
- Individual student does think-aloud in forum; other students help.
- Students do think-alouds individually; compare with others. (monitoring)
- Teacher or students do independent think-alouds orally, in writing, on an overhead, with Post-it notes, or in journal. (monitoring/independence)

Starting Points

There are several strategies, called general reading processes, that researchers have discovered successful readers use every time they read. If your students don't do these things, this is the place to start your think-aloud modeling since these strategies will have the greatest pay-off for them across all reading tasks. The chart below defines these general processes.

General Processes of Reading: What Good Readers Do Every Time They Successfully Read

- Activate background/continue to personally connect to content throughout reading (activate and bring your appropriate background knowledge about reading and content to the reading task; use existing life knowledge to make sense of new information; apply what you are learning to your own questions and concerns).

- Decode text into words and meanings (occurs at word, sentence, and text/genre levels).

- Set purpose for reading (think about whether you are reading for pleasure, to pursue an inquiry, for information, in order to converse with someone, in order to write, and so on, and read in an appropriate fashion to meeting your goals).

- Make predictions (create hypotheses and continually adjust them in light of new information).

- Visualize ("see" what you are reading; create a visual story world or mental model—with informational texts—that represents the meaning of the text).

- Ask questions (interrogate the text, the self, and the author before, during, and after reading).

- Summarize (bring meaning forward throughout the reading, determining what is important and continually synthesizing it with what has gone before).

- Monitor understanding/self-correct (continuously check that reading makes sense and use fix-it strategies when it doesn't).

- Reflect on meaning (consolidate knowledge with what was previously known).

- Prepare to apply what has been learned (create new knowledge structures, or schema, and ways of thinking and use these in new situations).

What Think-Alouds Can Do for Students: Opening the Window on Reading Strategies

The power of think-alouds was revealed to me when I was conducting the research that led to *You Gotta BE the Book* (Teachers College Press, 1997/2008). Hoping to better understand what accounted for the difference between expert and at-risk adolescent readers, I designed a study to examine these two kinds of readers. I discovered that the expert readers continuously and simultaneously used ten different dimensions of interpretive strategies and response strategies during any particular reading of narratives (see box opposite). These strategies included general reading processes but went well beyond these to include many text- and task-specific processes particular to reading narrative. The kids who had intense difficulties with reading, on the other hand, couldn't identify or use a single interpretive response strategy.

With this evidence before me, I asked: How can I help these poor readers? Where do I start? Knowing from the expert readers that visualizing and participating in textual worlds were two dimensions of response that were necessary to achieving response on other, more reflective dimensions, I chose these two strategies as a starting point. Using think-alouds, visual art, symbolic story representation, and drama/action strategies, I helped the poorer readers to visualize while they read and to participate in a story world—to experience it as a character, for example. Once this basic level of response was achieved, the students were much more able to use more reflective strategies, such as inferring and elaborating.

Illuminating the Importance of Visualizing

Visualizing, I discovered, was perhaps the most obvious characteristic of student response to any kind of text, so much so that I've written that "Reading is Seeing" and that visualizing should be added to the general processes. I've also devoted a section to helping kids visualize through think-alouds in Chapter 6.

From these students, I noticed that readers of narrative have the particular challenge of visualizing characters, settings, and events. Students who did not intensely visualize and participate in "story worlds" did not engage with the text in other dimensions. In other words, if we don't help kids visualize settings, characters, and action, then they will not be able to reflect on story action, the ways the story was construction, what the story means, the author's purpose and perspective, and a lot of other things that expert readers of narrative do.

General Processes and Visualization

The point is that even reading a narrative has task-specific demands, as exhibited in the box below. (Reading informational texts also requires visualization, a kind—albeit a different kind—of a mental model.)

Interdependent Dimensions of Literary Response for Reading Narrative

Entering the Story World

- Willingness to enter a story world.
- Entering the story world through interest in story action (and interest in character, setting, author, and other reasons).

Imagining the Story World

- Seeing the story world: visualizing settings, situations, and characters.
- Relating to characters: becoming, empathizing, and observing characters.

Extending and Connecting to the Story World

- Elaborating on the story world: noticing and inferring, embellishing and adding details, and creating new situations and episodes.
- Connecting: bringing and relating literature to one's life.

Reflecting on the Experienced Story World

- Reflecting on the significance of events (theme) and behavior (judging characters).
- Noticing and reflecting on the constructedness of text, including the author's use of literary conventions and why the author has constructed the text that way.
- Recognizing reading as a transaction includes recognizing and conversing with author, her meaning, and her vision.
- Evaluating the author and the self as a reader includes articulating understanding of one's own reading processes as part of that relationship.

(Wilhelm, 2008)

Navigating New Text Structures

Sometimes educators and the public can get lulled into thinking that "reading is reading" and that if kids can decode words they can read any kind of text, no matter the text structure or conventions. This works as long as texts are familiar, simple, and fairly similar. Things quickly fall apart once students read different text types like ironic monologues, fables, satires, arguments or classifications, or texts that incorporate particular conventional tasks such as interpreting graphs, diagrams, symbolism, or irony for which they need to recognize these new text features and use new kinds of reading strategies. This is why teaching reading at the upper elementary levels and beyond requires a focus on text- and task-specific reading strategies.

Let's say that you drive a Toyota Camry with a stick shift. Your friend drives a Mazda. You ask to borrow her car. She tosses you her keys, you jump in, turn the ignition, and away you go, largely without thinking. How are you able to do this? The cars are so similar that driving one is much like driving the other. (My thanks to Michael Smith for this example.) Similarly, a fourth grader can move effortlessly from one R.L. Stine novel to another, because the task of reading this text is similar enough to the author's other novels; the reader can automatically transfer her skills to this new situation. Or a student who can easily read a narrative on a literal level will be able to move from one story to another and succeed in reading on a literal level again.

But now let's say your friend wants you to help her move, and you find yourself behind the wheel of a moving van with three clutches. Yikes! Now you slow down. You start talking to yourself. "First put the key in the ignition" you might whisper to yourself, "depress the first clutch and turn the key…." If something goes wrong, like the engine chokes out, you'll say, "Okay, let the clutch out a bit slower now…."

What's happened is that the task has changed. You can use some of the same skills you used from your previous driving experience, but you have to adapt those skills to a different situation and you have to develop some new skills too. If you've never driven a vehicle with a clutch, then you will need someone to model or talk you through the task, and you will certainly take the language and expertise she has lent you to talk yourself through your own first few repetitions of shifting gears.

When I asked Josh to move from a literal level of reading *Monster* to an inferential and interpretive one, it was like asking him to get out of the Mazda and get behind the wheel of that big moving van. Most texts that students read from fifth grade through high school require some level of inferring, connecting of inferences, identification and judging of character and perspective, and main idea identification. Many of the reading skills they already possess need to be applied but some new skills also need to be awakened and exercised, particularly when the text conventions, structure, or genre is unfamiliar. Think-alouds help students take what they already know about reading and apply it to new reading situations. They also help students realize that in some cases they need to develop new skills for text that makes new kinds of demands.

Assisting and Empowering Struggling Readers

In two extended studies regarding the literate activity of boys (Smith and Wilhelm, 2002; 2006), I was struck by how much all of the boys expressed a desire for competence. They would go to great lengths to avoid tasks (like reading) that they did not feel they could competently complete. In classroom situations when think-alouds were provided that helped them successfully complete, or at least successfully approach and improve, their performance on a difficult task, they were much more willing to undertake it.

Many of the boys felt reading was drudgery and that they weren't very good at it. Think-alouds allowed me and other teachers to model our own enjoyment and show reading as a pleasurable pursuit. Think-alouds also highlighted the problem-solving activity of readers, and showed kids that even teachers make mistakes and have to correct them. Many of the boys thought that expert readers never make mistakes (perhaps a function of the fact that we teach books we've read many times, as Rabinowitz and Smith, 1998, suggest) and that their own struggles showed how poor they were as readers. Having boys use think-alouds had the added benefit of revealing students' unsuspected strengths. These strengths were made apparent and I could name and celebrate them with the students. Many of the kids were later able to deduce and name their own strengths, weaknesses, areas of confusion, and progress by using think-alouds.

Think-Alouds Help Students to...

Q&A 2: How do think-alouds help less experienced readers improve comprehension?

- **understand that reading should make sense!** (Poor readers concentrate on decoding words and often do not make meaning or expect texts to make sense.)

- **move beyond literal decoding to comprehending the global meanings of text.** (Poor readers have a limited, highly passive view of reading as simple decoding and acceptance of someone else's monolithic meaning. Expert readers understand that they do a lot of work with the text to responsively construct meaning and sense at both the local/sentence and global/whole text levels.)

- **learn how to read by using many different strategies in actual contexts of use.** (Poor readers have been shown to have a very impoverished idea of what reading really involves. They have a limited repertoire of strategies and may not be able to apply and use the strategies they possess in real reading contexts.)

- use particular strategies when reading particular text types. (National assessments show that many students master general strategies but do not understand that particular conventions and text types or genres often require additional strategies.)

- share ways of reading. In sharing with peers and teachers, students see that reading is an enjoyable social pursuit through which they can relate to one another about texts and ideas. (Poor readers see reading as a private, solitary pursuit rather than a social pursuit of conversing with authors, characters, and other readers. Much current research shows that teaching and learning are inherently social acts. Plus, Lev Vygotsky posited that two can often do together what neither can do alone. Reading together assists students.)

- learn about themselves and their own thinking and reading. This reflection helps students learn and use strategies on a self-conscious level. (This process is highly motivating particularly for students disenfranchised by school because their competence can be made evident by think-alouds. Poor readers are not aware of how they read and do not monitor and self-correct. Expert readers are able to analyze their thinking and reflect on their reading.)

Think-Alouds *For* and *As* Inquiry

Anchor Standards
for Reading, esp. 9
Anchor Standards
for Writing, 7–9

As an educator who has worked as a teacher from the elementary to graduate school levels, I know that learning through an inquiry approach is immensely beneficial for our students by increasing engagement, understanding, and achievement (see Wilhelm, 2007; Wilhelm, Wilhelm and Boas, 2008; Wilhelm and Novak, 2011). Many students, however, are not accustomed to learning through inquiry. How can we assist them in the transition from a focus on learning content through information transmission to learning and applying conceptual understandings through the use of higher-order thinking skills as is now required by the CCSS and the next generation of standards and assessments?

Think-alouds can help students progress toward thinking for themselves and engaging independently in all the phases of inquiry: problem definition, goal setting, task decomposition/devising investigations, reading, questioning at global and local levels, collecting data, organizing and analyzing data, supporting conclusions with evidence, and creating culminating projects that address the inquiry problem in some way. (All of these capacities are required by the CCSS.) Think-alouds make apparent the abstract processes of the students' own thinking as they make plans, rehearse processes, identify challenges and struggles, and ask questions out loud and practice answering them. A think-aloud is a form of inquiring into our own thinking that can guide students to test, expand, revise and ultimately justify their thinking.

As always, teachers first model the think-aloud process for students by articulating their own thinking during each phase of the inquiry. As students watch their teachers model the think-aloud process, they then move to the mentoring phase by helping the teacher with the think-aloud and then help peers engage in a similar process. Eventually, students can work in small groups, pairs, and on their own in the monitoring phase where they consolidate and demonstrate independence.

By frequently using think-alouds, we can make our classrooms into laboratories of learning, or metacognitive workshops, where we inquire not only to understand and apply what we have learned, but to get to the very process of inquiry, the process of learning how to learn.

By using think-alouds to model, mentor, and monitor students' reading, inquiry, and problem-solving processes, the classroom becomes a place where teachers and students engage in joint inquiry into major issues, learn major concepts and procedures together and apply these to the inquiry at hand. Teachers become master inquirers, actually doing the discipline rather than merely receiving or talking about it. And students become apprentices who are helped into the collaborative inquiry that is the basis of all disciplines and at the heart of all true understanding and wisdom. Together, through inquiry, teachers and students take the journey of true learning together.

When students learn to infer, they can successfully engage and make meaning with texts that have a high inference load. Figuring out the puzzle of meaning keeps them from wanting to put the book down!

As they engage in this journey, students come to understand the substance, process, and form of disciplinary knowledge, gaining understanding into how such knowledge is created, structured, expressed, and used. I would argue that this is the end goal we should have for our students. They should be able to identify: what I know, how I know, how I can justify what I know, and how I can learn more. This is the process of inquiry.

Heading Down the River

I began and end this chapter with a learning story that takes place on a river. Though I've enjoyed canoeing since I was a kid, I've become a passionate white-water kayaker over the last twelve years. There are many canoeing skills that transfer, but there are many additional task-specific expectations in kayaking. I would have to adapt some of my previous skills to meet the demands of kayaking, and I would have to learn some new special skills. One of these would be the Eskimo roll, since white water kayakers often turn over and need to be righted quickly.

Unlike many of my reading students, I was already motivated to learn this new skill. I was eager to learn kayaking. I like outdoor sports and have lots of friends with whom I could pursue this sport. When we teach reading, it's helpful to make it something akin to kayaking: an adventure we will undertake together that will be challenging, requiring us to learn and use new strategies but that will be fun, social, and will get us somewhere.

When I first got in a kayak, the teacher did not immediately send me through rapids where I would have been sure to capsize. We worked for several sessions in a heated pool, learning how to get out of an overturned boat, how to "eddy out" of a river's current to get a rest, and how to do a variety of strokes—some highly specific to kayaking—that are important on a river. All of these tools or strategies were explicitly taught in a situation that helped everyone in the class to be successful.

Nonetheless, I was surprised at how frustrated I became with learning the Eskimo roll. It was obvious to me and everyone else in the class that I could not get my kayak turned back over. I was the "remedial" student. Even though the class was highly supportive, the instruction appropriate, and my motivation high, I felt like quitting. I didn't understand why my competence as a canoeist was not translating to the kayak. The reason, of course, was the new task-specific expectations of the challenge. It occurred to me how much more difficult it is for our struggling readers who do not believe that reading can be fun, don't value it, and have behind them a lifetime of bailing out of their reading "boats."

My teacher didn't give up on me. He arranged for an extra session, guided my paddle to the correct position as I hung upside down under the water, and provided advice and language to "help you think and talk your way through it…. When you get turned over, set up, scratch your butt with the paddle end, look at your other paddle face, then kick your knee and roll your head toward your knee!" He had me recite these steps. He gave me some videotapes to watch of expert kayak rollers. Though I was far behind the rest of the class on rolling, one day I had a breakthrough! I hit four rolls in a row! Boy, was I excited! After a while, I was hitting 100 percent of my rolls in a pool. I had reached a new zone of actual development.

Then it was off to the river. This was a new zone of proximal development. The first few times that I turned over, I didn't even try to roll, I just got out of that dad-blamed boat as quickly as possible—I wasn't too happy with the rocks going by my head, the cold water, the lack of oxygen, and the roaring water.

Luckily, my patient teacher was still supporting me. The next time we went to the river, he made me do several rolls in a quiet eddy. I was successful. "Now," he said, "I want you to go into the current, roll over on purpose, and give it a try." This was a whole new set of demands and I had trouble. So we made adjustments. After a while I did a few successful rolls. I'll never forget successfully rolling over in heavy current, with water cascading out of my helmet, yelling, "What's the problem? Because there is NO PROBLEM!!!"

Then he told me, "It will be harder still when you go over by surprise. At least make the attempt to roll. Just get it in your head that you won't bail out unless you've tried to roll twice!" (Think how powerful it would be if we could get our readers to try several self-correction strategies before they gave up on their reading! See Chapter 4 for more on that!)

Well, it's 12 years down the road—or, should I say, the *river* of life. I have paddled many of the major rivers and canyons in the West. I have done many class V drops and self-support trips that take days or weeks at a time out in the wilderness where there is no help to be had if one screws up. I have confidence in myself, and it is very rare that I miss my first attempt at a roll. When I have a problem, I can talk my way to a solution. I have internalized much of my teacher's expertise and can use it to identify and solve problems. Kayaking is a physical and cognitive skill that provides immediate feedback to the practitioner. If you aren't rolling your kayak it's pretty obvious. Reading is harder still. We need to be the kind of teachers that my kayak teacher is, constantly guiding and adapting instruction that is appropriate and contextualized. We need to recognize that being able to read one kind of text (or paddle one kind of boat) doesn't mean that you can read a different kind of text.

We need to remember that reading (even more so than kayaking!) is hard work, that teaching kids to read is hard work and will require constant attention, support, and adaptations. Even with good teaching, plan on small gains over time that will come in fits and starts. Though progress may seem slow and may even seem to regress at times, learning will be occurring, and one day you will find your students at the bottom of several rapids… or readings… that they can look back at and proudly say, "I read that!" Maybe they will even do some fist pumps and yell "What is the problem?! Because there IS NOT A PROBLEM?" They will have learned something new, and they will be able to do that something on their own for the rest of their lives. And let's not forget that though learning to read may be one of the most difficult and challenging achievements in a human lifetime, being a good reader is intensely fun and leads to more and more learning and more and more fun as we proceed down the "reading river" of life. We need to know this and work towards this. So do our students.

CHAPTER 3

WHAT ALL GOOD READERS DO

Introducing General Reading-Process Think-Alouds

n the last chapter, I reviewed the basic processes that all competent readers use every time they read. These are the general strategies—predicting, visualizing, and so on—that give us the biggest bang for the strategic buck. Since every successful reader uses all of these strategies every time they read anything, this is where we need to first put our energy: making sure all of our students have mastered all the general processes. This is necessary but insufficient to expert reading. Even if students can use all the general processes, nearly any reading experience will also require learning the task and text-specific processes I'll cover in later chapters. Because this set of general strategies is used by all competent readers with the reading of any text, it is a perfect strategy set to focus on as

CCSS

Anchor Standards
for Reading,
1–6, 10

you incorporate think-alouds into your teaching of reading and the specific content of particular texts.

To show you how I plan and conduct a general-process think-aloud, and then follow it up with different kinds of think-aloud practice, let me introduce you to a motley crew of sixth graders who chose to study the future of planet Earth. After some discussion we settled on the essential question: "What will the future be like?" with the subquestion: "Who and what will survive?" Their reasons for taking on this theme ranged from the altruistic: "I want to know how I can help make things like pollution and global warming better," to the practical, "Old people today don't know much about computers and other modern stuff, and I guess it's not their fault that they were born so long ago, but I want to think about my future and how technology will influence that," to my pride-slashing favorite, "Mr. Wilhelm, I want to know what life will be like for me when I'm old like you!"

With my delusions of remaining youthfully hip effectively banished, I decided to begin the unit with a shared reading of Gloria Skurzynski's *Virtual War*. I chose this novel because it is engaging and short. It paints a portrait of the fairly immediate future, which could shape our discussions. In the book everyone lives in domed cities due to nuclear fallout, and war for a few remaining safe havens is fought "virtually" over computers. The heroes of the story are teens who have been trained by electronic mentors since birth to engage in this virtual war. Though it's written for young adults, the book has a moderate inference load and deals with some heavy issues regarding personal freedom, genetic engineering, the environment, war, and violence.

Now I'll tease out the steps I took to plan and use think-alouds to teach some general process strategies.

General Process Strategies (Steps 1-8)

STEP 1: Choose a short section of text (or a short text)

Choose a text or excerpt that is interesting to students, ideally with content that links to a current inquiry project. The text segment ought to be in students' ZPDs by presenting some particular challenges to most of your students. Remember that Vygotsky said learning can only occur in the ZPD, so we want a text that students can read with your help, but that would give them significant difficulty on their own.

It works well to use the first page or two of a longer text with a think-aloud. Struggling readers tend to give up within the first few paragraphs; helping them to understand these passages gets them off to a strong start. And this helps orient all students to the kind of text it is, the vocabulary that will be used, and tips them off to the strategies they'll probably need to continue. Of course, it's also great to work with a complete and coherent piece of text, such as a short story (particularly if it's only a few pages) or a chapter (again, if not too lengthy). I've also had success teaching various conventions and text types with comics, sections of graphic novels, YouTube videos, poems and the like (see Smith and Wilhelm, 2010, for examples).

Give each student a copy of the text. I usually introduce the first think-alouds by photocopying or typing the text on the left-hand side of a sheet, and providing notebook lines on the right side on which they will write their responses to the text (see "The Chaser" example, page 77). Providing the lines reminds kids that I want them to respond moment by moment and line by line, and that their reading "moves" are in response to particular codes or writing "moves" that the author placed in the text.

Once students get the hang of it, they can simply put their notebooks next to their reading and record their responses there. I also have students use sticky notes to record their think-aloud responses. If you can't do the typing or photocopying, put the text on transparency sheets and model your own think-aloud using the overhead projector or SMART board.

STEP 2: Decide on a few strategies to highlight

Explain to students how a think-aloud works and what strategies you will be trying out (choose one or a few related strategies for best results). Also brainstorm why and how these strategies will be helpful to them in their own reading, right now and in the future.

With *Virtual War*, I primarily spotlighted one strategy: predicting and correcting predictions. I focused particularly on predicting future action and making predictions about characters: what they were like and what they would do. (Making character predictions merges with inferring character, which might be considered a more text-specific strategy of reading narratives, but I focus on it here as a more general strategy of predicting). I felt that the kids were ready to consider how authors construct stories to lead us on, create interest and suspense. Since our unit was about the future, the whole notion of making predictions and adjusting our behavior to discourage or encourage our predictions to come true seemed very central to our study. The students were also ready to consider how authors create character and how the concept of character is emphasized in this novel; the teens' characters are shaped by genetic mutation and reared by computer programs.

To summarize, I decided to focus on prediction because I felt it was in the students' zone of proximal development, because it was necessary to our unit of study, and because the plot of this text, like our unit, is in a sense one big prediction about what life will be like in the not-so-distant future. I knew that during the unit we would try to surmise various authors' predictions about the future and converse with the authors and each other about these, which is another important set of reading skills and a springboard that can lead us to more future reading and inquiry.

STEP 3: State your purposes

In this case, I would tell students that the purposes of reading *Virtual War* are to

Anchor Standards for Reading, 6, 9, 10

Anchor Standards for Writing, 7–10

- enjoy a really good story about kids in the future who are just a bit older than they are.

- get us started on our agreed upon inquiry into the future (these first two goals pertain to setting purposes for reading, a general-process strategy).

- learn some strategies that will help us in our inquiry, namely, making and adjusting predictions, and understanding how character is formed both in the real world and in the story world the author has created, so that we can enter into characters' experiences and predict what they might do and feel.

Tell students that as you are thinking aloud, you want them to pay attention to the strategies you use so they can explain what, why, how, and when you used them. This is wonderful for sharpening their attention!

What the Research Says

Studies of teaching generally show that trying to do more than three things at once distracts student attention from all of the elements. It's better to focus and really address a few goals rather than diffusing energy by trying to address too many. Kids can easily be overwhelmed by "sensory overload!" as one of my middle school students likes to say. Start where the students are and focus on one or two new strategies that they are ready to learn and use. Once students are familiar with think-alouds and have mastered the highlighted strategies, then you can cast a wider net and progress to a focus on more sophisticated strategies, one or two at a time.

STEP 4: Read the text aloud to students and think-aloud as you do so

I read the text slowly and stop quite often to report out, doing my best to target the focus strategies of predicting and inferring character, though other general strategies like asking questions naturally kick in too. When I report out during the first few think-alouds, I put the text down, look at students, and say "Hmmm…" to signal that I am shifting from reading to thinking aloud. First, I preview the book, wondering aloud about the title, the cover illustrations, the back cover, and so on. "Hmmm. I predict this book will be about a war fought on computers, like a computer game. [Looking at cover illustration] Hmmm. I see three people, but their heads don't fit their bodies and they are on a computer screen with computer code. I bet these are the people who will fight the virtual war, or maybe they are 'knowbots' who will fight the war on-screen. I predict that they are really smart and that is why their heads are so big. One of them looks younger than the others and mutated or something. They all have boxes around their necks… I bet that's important but I don't know why." When a teacher says aloud all he is noticing and doing as he reads, students finally "see" the steps and motions of an expert reader.

Text	Think-Aloud
The sky was golden.	Hmmm. I know the first lines of text are important and I should notice them. This one's funny—skies aren't usually gold. I wonder if this means he's happy, or it's a great day or something.
Corgan could feel sand beneath his fingers. What were those trees called, he wondered, the tall ones that curved to the sky?	Hmmm. I predict he means palm trees. But why doesn't he know the name? He doesn't sound very well informed or experienced.

Text	Think-Aloud
What does it matter, he thought. Things don't need names. They haven't told me the names of lots of things, and I don't really care. It's nice to lie here like this under the sky and the trees and not have to practice for a while.	Hmmm. Who are these "they"? They must be people who teach or control Corgan. These "they" must make him practice all the time… I bet they are making him practice to fight the virtual war. He seems to accept the way things are since he says "I don't really care." Or maybe he does care but he can't do anything about it. I'll have to read further to find out. I wonder if it will be like the movie *The Matrix*? I think it's weird that he doesn't know the names of things. I wonder why "they" are withholding information from him.
A girl walked across the beach… and his LiteSuit began to shimmer with the color of blood.	Hmm. I wonder if that's because she's beautiful. I predict that the LiteSuit reflects his mood or feelings because if his LiteSuit turns red and shimmers I bet that means he is excited or interested by her. Things shimmer when they are excited or stimulated.
Corgan knew what blood looked like. Once, a few months ago, as he'd walked along the tunnel from his Box to his Clean Room, a tile fell from the ceiling and hit his hand. His knuckles had bled, the first and only time he had ever seen real blood.	Hmmm. There sure is a lot on this first page! This is weird. Why has he only seen blood once? I predict that he must be totally protected… I bet that he is special in some way; I can't imagine that they would spend that much attention on everybody, plus he must be one of the main characters of this book.
The way the Supreme Council had carried on it was as if Corgan's arm had been chopped off or something.	Hmmm. Who is the Supreme Council? The "they"? I don't know. I predict that they might be the people playing at the Virtual War. I predict that they are certainly the people who are controlling Corgan. I predict that there must be a lot of contamination and sickness if they worry about a little cut. Corgan must be really special in some way and being protected, probably to fight the Virtual War. I'll bet that's it.

I continue thinking aloud for another page before cycling on to the next step. Notice that I name certain text features (title, illustration, the importance of the first few lines of text), and explain why I'm looking especially close at them to help me make sense of things. As you report out, demonstrate the way expert readers notice text features and interpret these (see Rules of Notice, page 83). Use verbs like, I wonder, I think, I predict, I bet, I'm confused to spotlight the kinds of mental moves you are making. Use phrases like I'm going to reread, or I'll have to read further, or I don't know—to both highlight reading strategies and show kids that as an expert reader stitches together an understanding of a new text, it's okay that he has some loose threads—it's okay that he doesn't know, that his thinking is tentative, that he is going to have to read on, think and reflect to find out. That's what predictions are—best guesses that we suspend in our heads, that the text will either prove were on target or in need of correction.

STEP 5: Have students underline the words and phrases that helped you use a strategy

For example, after completing my think-aloud of the first two pages of *Virtual War*, I have my students underline the phrases that they think helped me infer about character (primarily Corgan) and make predictions about his situation. We then talk about exactly how Gloria Skurzynski—and by extension, other authors—introduce characters and begin painting a portrait of their personalities. We also talk about foreshadowing, how authors lay hints about future action so that we can predict and anticipate what may happen next, feel suspense, and perhaps be tricked—through the proverbial "red herrings."

As I continue to read aloud, the students underline clues to future action: they underline details about the Go-Ball match with the beautiful girl Sharla, and predict that it was a test for the Virtual War; they underline a description of how Corgan was distracted by Sharla and predict that the enemy in the *Virtual War* will also try to distract him. When Mendor, Corgan's teacher, enters the scene, the students are able to confirm these predictions and learn that the Virtual War is only 17 days away and that Corgan will be the one to fight it.

I like to have students make predictions and underline the clues that led to their predictions. After reading a section, students can go back and see whether their predictions were borne out, proven wrong, or remain inconclusive. Stephanie Harvey (2000) suggests that students go back after reading to code their predictions with A+ if it came true, A– if it did not, and a "0" if the evidence is inconclusive.

STEP 6: List the cues and strategies used

After I have done some thinking aloud with students using a particular strategy, I ask them to make a list of the signals that prompt us to use the strategy. Authors create character, for example, through details about a character's looks, diction, thoughts, clothing, actions, friends, comments from others, favorite surroundings, and so on. They expect us to notice, interpret and piece together these cues to infer character. I then ask students which cues they used or underlined and which they did not. Then I ask them to continue using the cues they did and to make a renewed effort to attend to cues they did not use yet.

I like to keep the lists of such cues on an anchor chart posted on the classroom wall. (See Smith and Wilhelm, 2010, for a complete list of cues for inferring character.)

STEP 7: Ask students to identify other situations (real world and reading situations) in which they could use these same strategies

Anchor Standards for Language, 5

Anchor Standards for Reading, 4

Research on reflection (e.g. Edmiston, 1991) shows that asking students in the midst of an activity (or immediately after) what strategies they are using and how they could be used in other situations helps students learn and transfer these strategies to other contexts.

General-process strategies are used in particular ways during reading, but they also mirror parallel operations in real life. For instance, we often must summarize activity, monitor how we are doing, make predictions, or infer character. All of these strategies inform not only our judgments, but our decisions and actions. In order to connect the strategy to my students' lived experience, I will segue from predictions to the topic of the future that we are studying. Why do we need to predict things about the future? How does that help us? Who tries to predict the future and how do they try to do it? How do people try to predict or plan their own personal futures? Why is that important? How well do different prediction strategies work? What evidence are such predictions based on?

Progressing to characterization, I might now ask my sixth graders such questions as: How do you decide what a person is like? How do you determine if you like a person when you first meet him? And, why are first impressions so important? What are some things you notice as you interpret first impressions? Or I'll ask them about me—what they've noticed, and why it's important to figure out what I'm like.

Then they can brainstorm other textual and real life situations, as well as people who are important to figure out and make predictions about.

STEP 8: Reinforce the think-aloud with follow-up lessons

The "eighth step"—and it's a crucial one—is to extend and consolidate the strategies introduced in the initial think-aloud. A new strategy requires guidance and practice to internalize. You can provide this both by using the same text to do more think-alouds with the strategy, or with a new text. It is important to continue practicing and reflecting on the strategies to consolidate mastery for independent use.

Following are a few teaching techniques my colleagues and I have had success with. You'll only use some of these activities some of the time, but you will want to have all these tools in your tool kit. They work well with any of the types of think-alouds discussed in this book. I've organized them generally along the Vygotskian teaching continuum, so you will get a sense of how you might use them to gradually remove the scaffolded assistance and release responsibility for the strategy use to the student. However, most of the techniques could be adapted to fit on various points of that continuum.

Consider This

Before linking the think-aloud process to reading, you may wish to have students think aloud with something more concrete and accessible to them. Have them do a think-aloud for a physical task with which they are familiar. The possibilities are endless: I've had kids do this for splitting wood, fly casting, programming a DVD, turning on e-mail, mailing a letter, creating a Facebook page, carving a ski turn, cooking spaghetti, even for making a peanut butter sandwich.

- Tell them that the think-aloud is for someone who doesn't know how to do the activity. I ask them to tape-record the

think-aloud as they actually engage in the process. Kids could also write it out, of course.

- Ask them to first state the purpose of the activity, then describe how they prepare and get started. Then they can record everything that they think, notice, and do as they engage in the activity, as well as how they reflect on and evaluate their performance.

- Afterward, ask the class to discuss what we can learn about an activity by doing a think-aloud as we engage in it versus after it, and what we learn by listening to someone else talk through a task.

Teacher Does/Student Watches

Modeling—And More Modeling

Do lots of short teacher-modeled think-alouds, particularly of new strategies. Use real texts of immediate interest so that modeling is always done in the context of meaningful reading. Then gradually release responsibility over to the students. Remember the fishing practice of "catch and release"—students should catch the new strategy, or the full repertoire of strategies needed to approach a text, before you release them to angle the text on their own.

Teacher Does/Students Help

Think-Alongs/Mentoring

As you read aloud and think aloud, students follow along. A good way to introduce this is to have students identify and say aloud the kinds of moves and strategies you report on, and explain why these are useful and important. This can be done by pairs of students so everyone is involved. They literally "think along" with you and articulate what it is you are doing and why, immediately after you report on a particular move. As they improve, they can identify the prompts that show a particular move should be made. For example, I was recently reading *Pobby and Dingan* with fourth graders. This is a wonderfully written and offbeat young adult book out of Australia. (It does contain some strong language, but the students I was working with absolutely loved it.) It's about the reality of two imaginary friends and what happens to a family, particularly a callow older brother, when his younger sister's two imaginary friends go missing in an opal mine because of the family's carelessness. As I read the first passage about how Kellyanne's imaginary friends Pobby and Dingan are "maybe-dead," I thought aloud, "I wonder what has happened to them? I bet this story is starting here and will flash back to explain what has happened to Pobby and Dingan. I'll bet something bad has happened to Kellyanne and that has made her feel like her imaginary friends have left her." My fourth graders immediately identified my moves as "wonderings" or "lots of predictions." I then told them my first prediction was one about story construction as I guessed that this story was starting in the middle of something. My other prediction concerned story content— about what actually would happen in the story. When I asked the kids why I had made this move, one fourth grader said, "The author is starting in the middle because he wants us to wonder what happened. And we know it must be something bad for them to be 'maybe-dead,' so we make predictions and it makes us want to read more to find out if we are right!"

Teacher Does/Students Do

Strategies Lists/More Mentoring!

Together with students, create a list of the strategies you're using and post it on an anchor chart as a reference for students. Students can use this list to guide their own strategy use, to identify strategies they are using, to identify strategies that weren't used but could have been, and so forth. Sometimes students will make an effort to come up with a new strategy to add to the list.

Posting these lists around the classroom can serve as a reminder to students of what things they are supposed to do when they read. It becomes a kind of contextual mentoring or environmental assistance embedded in the classroom. Students can build from these lists to devise symbols for various strategies to facilitate self-assessment. They can then code others' or their own think-alouds to see what strategies they are using and not using.

Based on our discussions of my think-alouds, we created a class list of foreshadowing clues (e.g., "story starts in middle—have to figure out what happened before!" "there is a problem—how will it get fixed?" "maybe-dead" "not knowing makes you want to find out!"), prediction moves ("wonder what happened before" "guess what will happen next" "figure out what the story is really about"), and reasons to predict ("makes you want to read and find out what happens" "helps you think about what is happening" "makes suspense!" "like a game—see if you are right!").

Anchor Standards for Reading, 1–6

We talked about why predictions were such an important move at the beginning of a text, and then proceeded to think about other moves I had made in my think-alouds over the first few pages of *Pobby and Dingan*. Our list was then expanded to look like this:

- wonder about what happened before

- predict what will happen next

- make guesses about what's uncertain

- figure out who characters are and what they are like (by reading inner thoughts, expressions, feelings, how they look, what they say, etc.)

- figure out why characters are doing what they are doing (especially why Kellyanne has imaginary friends!) (study behaviors and figure out probable motives)

- see the house in your mind (pretty weird, with car doors between rooms!), and the town and the opal mine. (look for details about the setting, visualize it in your mind, and figure out what it would be like to be there)

Read Aloud/Pause/Write (More Mentoring)

As you think-aloud, pause at certain points, have students write down what they are thinking and doing at that point in the text, and then take turns sharing your moves. For example, in Chapter 2, Kellyanne's dad takes Pobby and Dingan to his opal mine and promises to take good care of them. I paused, and the students and I wrote down what we were thinking. Most of them correctly predicted that dad would lose Pobby and Dingan and upset Kellyanne. For those who did not make this prediction we noted the clues the successful predictors had used. For example, dad had gone overboard assuring Kellyanne that her imaginary friends would be fine, and because dad appeared to have forgotten about them when he arrived back home. With this activity, students can compare their strategies to yours and to those of their peers. They will discover that there are many ways to get meaning from a text and that every reading is unique. They will learn that some strategies and readings are not as appropriate and rich as others—but perhaps more importantly, they will borrow and adapt strategies to suit their needs.

Talk-Throughs/More Mentoring!

With this one, students "talk through" their reading response as I pause while reading a section of text aloud. This provides great "scaffolding" in preparation for when I will ask them to read and talk through/write down their own reading activity. It's simpler for them because I am doing the reading, so they are able to concentrate on responding to the piece. I usually read, pause, and ask students to write down their responses to the passage I have read, and then have just one or two students read aloud what they wrote. At other times, I'll ask all students to jump in with their thinking as soon as I'm done reading a passage. Perhaps we'll go around the class, or perhaps we will play "Just Jump In," for which every student knows they have to take two turns sometime during the activity. (Sometimes I ask kids to stand and they are allowed to sit once they have made a contribution. I also sometimes give kids two objects which they deposit in a basket when they contribute. They know that they have to get rid of both objects during the think-aloud.)

Once students understand the gist of how think-alouds work through such shared activities, I then ask them to read and do their think-aloud responses on their own.

Students Do/Teacher Helps

Response Forum/More Mentoring!

With a forum (also known as a fishbowl), I start a think-aloud and then ask a student volunteer to "take the stage" by taking over the think-aloud for a short period. I might take over again for a while before asking for another volunteer, depending on whether there is something I want to model. The student who takes the stage is usually at the front or middle of the classroom, where she can be observed by the forum—the class or small group. (I prefer working in groups of four to six students, but it can be done as a whole-class activity.) When a think-aloud segment is over, other students may jump in to comment. To give comments from the forum some structure, I like to use the PQP format

- first, some Praise for the think aloud
- then, some Questions about the think aloud
- finally, some Polish suggestions—corrections, additions, and the like—OR Wonderings—"I wonder what would happen if you tried… or noticed…"

Or use the Law and Order format

- First, give L comments—something you Liked about the think-aloud, or something you learned from it.
- Then, W comments—something you Wondered about the think-aloud.
- Finally, O comments—friendly "Orders" you'd like to have the reader try, suggestions you might have for them the next time they do a think-aloud.

I think these kinds of prompts and guidelines help all students to voice a response and encourage them to make comments that are productive, varied, and that help the class celebrate a text as well as set goals for future reading challenges. Otherwise, I often find that my students do not make constructive comments and that they particularly avoid providing suggestions for improvement. To reinforce the importance of helping each other, I sometimes conclude my lessons by having students ask each other: "I wonder what would happen if you… [tried to do/use a particular strategy]" as a gentle way of making a suggestion.

At other times, though, you'll want the forum to "just jump in" to report out on the passage, so they can bounce their ideas off the student who's onstage. As we work through a text in this manner, we create a "group mosaic" or group think-aloud of various people's responses. This is a dynamic way to begin turning over the task to students. Your presence and the collaborative nature of this work provide a safety net that helps guide students to evermore independent performance.

Students Do/Teacher Watches and Assesses

Thought Bubbles/Monitoring

Some students take to think-alouds immediately, instantly knowing what you mean when you describe thinking about thinking or thinking about reading. They may already be using the strategies you highlight, even if they haven't named them or manipulated them. Thinking aloud extends their capacities and allows them to name them, think with them, manipulate, and extend them. Other students don't have any experience with metacognition, and may not have ever used the strategies you are spotlighting. Such students may be less willing to think out loud. For these students, "thought bubbles" are just the ticket. I draw a picture of a reader with a thought bubble above his or her head. For fun students might even draw their own picture, paste a school picture of themselves on the face, and so forth. I'll make several copies of each picture so that students can use them to record several think-aloud moves. Then I ask them to write something they are thinking into the thought bubbles at various points in the text. When a thought bubble is filled, or when they move on to a different section of text, they then use a new thought bubble.

For example, at the end of Chapter 2 of *Pobby and Dingan*, the father has been arrested for "ratting" or trespassing on another miner's opal claim while he was looking for the missing imaginary friends. Kellyanne's brother, Ashmol, ends the chapter by thinking "of Dad and if he was in prison and how the whole thing was Pobby and Dingan's fault. And then I tried to get my head round how it could be their fault if they didn't even exist."

Jazzy, who had not spoken yet during the class, filled out her thought bubble by writing, "They are real because people act like they are real. And that is how it is everybody's fault." Jazzy was then asked to explain her comments and how this judging of characters was helping her as she read. Completing several—say five to ten— thought bubbles usually successfully ushers more reluctant readers into using think-alouds more independently. It's also a great transition to the techniques of visual think-alouds, described in Chapter 5.

Open Mind/Monitoring

With this extension, pairs of students complete the think-aloud as a whole group (or begin a new one with a new text), with one person reading aloud and pausing, and the other reporting out. Then students switch roles. The benefit? Students support each other, and can then widen their repertoire of strategy use by sharing their work with another pair or the larger group. I encourage students to get started by "opening their mind." If they have trouble, I tell them to just say whatever is happening in their mind. Even if they say "This is boring!" or "I don't know what to do," this is a start, and gives you valuable information about their level of awareness and response to the reading. You may learn that you have to do more work to get them engaged in the content of the text, e.g. by providing more frontloading, or help them to use a strategy of some kind to get started. If they truly do not understand the strategy or its use, it is important to get this kind of feedback so that you can intervene.

Flag the Text/Monitoring

Using Post-it notes as a tool for comprehension monitoring is common. I first learned about this nearly 20 years ago in the National Writing Project, and have had many colleagues, like Kelly Chandler, "The queen of Post-its," who have used these sticky pieces of paper in many creative ways.

Post-its can be very useful with think-alouds. For example, if students are reading a text-book that they can't write in, they can always record their thoughts on Post-its, sticking them right on the text as they respond. Or, it works very well to have small groups of students read the same story and then pool their Post-its onto one copy. If I give each student different-colored Post-its, they can see the similarities and differences in the number and types of strategies group members used. Sometimes I ask students to use particular colors for a particular strategy use, for instance one color for predictions, another for personal connections, and a third for visualizations. In this way, students can see at a glance how often they use each strategy and how the strategies are integrated throughout a story. Most software packages now have a sticky note function which can be used to post notes on electronic texts.

When you're finished reading a story, students can collect the Post-its in order and create a response timeline of their reading of a text. I usually have them do this on a roll of butcher paper that we hang in the classroom. Sometimes I post the pages of a story in order, spacing them a foot or so apart. Students attach their response around the appropriate page, perhaps drawing a line from their Post-it to the words or phrases that stimulated that response. At other times, I might just write the major events or details on the bottom of the butcher paper and let the students attach their Post-its above the events or details they responded to. There are obviously various ways to do this.

As a great way to have kids self-assess their strategy use, have them collect and classify Post-its from one or several texts they've read. For example, when Jazzy collected her thought bubbles halfway through our reading of *Pobby and Dingan*, she noticed that she had only eight Post-its (which was relatively few) and almost all of her comments were judgments about character. "I'm always telling them they are wrong or making a mistake or something. Or sometimes, I am trying to make them feel better like Kellyanne." After we had celebrated what a useful strategy this is (trying to be a help-mate or "agent" for a character, something many expert readers do), I asked Jazzy if there were other strategies she could try to use more often. "I think I could make more predictions about what they might do once they figure out their mistakes," she told me.

Like any other think-aloud record, students' Post-it responses become valuable resources for when they write about a piece of literature or their reading process. For example, my students use this raw material when I ask them to write a process analysis of how they read something.

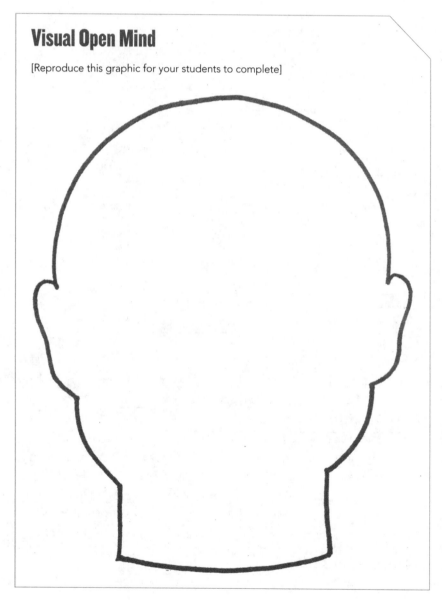

Visual Open Mind

[Reproduce this graphic for your students to complete]

Students can also draw or write in their thoughts on sticky notes while reading a particular passage. The picture could be devoted to a particular strategy or divided into sections prompting particular kinds of strategies, questions, etc.

Written Analyses of Reading <u>Heart of a Champion</u> and <u>With the Vikings</u> by Phil (5th grade)

Think-Aloud prompt personal connection; expression of interest

understands action and subtext

think-aloud practice taught Phil that it's good to engage emotionally with text

notices repetition and relationship to theme

Judges character

notices surprise—how his expectations weren't met and what this means

evaluates constructedness of text and relationship to story meaning

I was reading *Nighthoops* and some other Carl Deuker books and I liked it because I like basketball and it wasn't like most books that are boring and where not too much happens. *Nighthoops* had lots of action and it wasn't all about basketball. It was about making friends with a guy who was wild and needed help but it was all related to the basketball. It all had a relationship to the game. I liked that, everything hung together, so I thought I would read another one.

When I started reading *Heart of a Champion*, the first thing I noticed was that his dad had died. I kind of wondered what that would have to do with the book. Then I read that his dad was a golfer and wanted Seth to golf too, and Seth would do whatever other people wanted him to do. That really bugged me. And with his dad gone, he could do more of what he wanted, and this was how he got into baseball. And I was kind of mad about that, that he couldn't make his own decisions and all that.

But then this doing what other people wanted kept getting him in trouble. I noticed that this was like the major thing in the book. Like this older kid wanted him to drink, and Seth just took it, but his friend wouldn't do it so then Seth wouldn't do it either and I thought why can't you just make up your own mind? And later on he started drinking because there is always pressure, isn't there? At the end of the book his friend Jimmy died from drinking and driving. And they dedicated the next game to Jimmy and they won. But then they lost the next game. That surprised me and I put a big exclamation mark on my think-aloud post it. Then I was thinking that the author was showing that if you have a big life problem you can't just solve it and la la la everything gets fixed. You have to really work hard to stay out of trouble and to get out of trouble once you are in it.

After I thought about it I liked how the season ended so quick and unexpected, just like Jimmy dying, when they thought things would keep on going. All through the book, good things followed the bad things, except at the end. I think that showed how some mistakes are so big that you can't fix them, you just have to live with them.

So how did I read this? I read it being totally in to the story and the baseball, but I really started caring and following the characters, and judging them. Then later on I started thinking about the author and why the author did things the way he did, especially when he started surprising me towards the end and things didn't turn out how I thought. I was sad at the end, almost a little disappointed. Jimmy was a great guy but he ruined his life. What a waste, and he hadn't even learned from his dad's mistakes because his dad was an alcoholic. I just thought of this. The game tied his life together. He always did his best in games. But he wouldn't do his best in life. Why not? He could get up for the game but not for life? So he was a champion in the game but not in life. I guess that's what I like about these books, they wrap everything together.

expresses a relationship to and evaluation of author

his think-aloud and his writing help him achieve a sense of coherence

With the Vikings

I read this different than I read the Heart of a Champion. I didn't find it half as interesting. It wasn't about something I like to do or that I like. I mean it was so old. It had nothing to do with me. I guess I want what I read to be about me and my life. I mean I had a choice but it had to be about history and history is history.

I basically was reading the other book [Heart of a Champion] for enjoyment and for the story. This I was reading for information which I automatically think of as boring. I had to write this picture book for my reading buddy so I had to find stuff that would be interesting to her. So I took notes. Whenever I found something sort of interesting, I would make a note so I would remember. When I was done I felt relieved. Like I felt, good, that's done, now I can write the book. It was like this was something I had to do to do something else. The other book the point was reading. Here the point was researching and learning and then writing. I like writing, but here it was the topic that bugged me. I liked making the book though, that was cool. Especially the pictures and the pictures in the books I read really helped with that, to get the pictures right.

Phil shows an awareness that books of different genres require different stances (see chapter 6) and strategies

assesses self as a reader

cites strategy for remembering and placeholding important information

remembers purpose

visualized meaning by using visual cues

Fiona tells her reading group about the clues she used to make predictions during her reading. Her contribution is used to help compile a class list.

In fact, my students, like all adolescents, enjoy perusing these artifacts of their thinking, or more to the point, love this kind of self-analysis! (One student informed me "To know me is to love me!" I asked him why he was so sure. His reply: "I know myself really well and I really love myself.")

General Reading Strategies: Student Prompts

As you create your own lessons, use the following list of reading strategies and prompts as a checklist.

First, some management tips:

- You could go through the strategies in the order presented, but you don't have to. And you don't have to go through all the strategies; you should focus on what you think your students most need. If your students are mostly adept at predicting, for example, you would not take the time to do a whole-class think-aloud on predicting.

- When I introduce these general processes to my students, I do it by introducing a couple at a time with short texts. We put the strategies and prompts on chart paper and post them with illustrations at the front of the classroom.

I. Set Purposes for Reading

There is a host of research that shows how vitally important it is to model purpose-setting for kids. When students don't have a personal purpose for reading, they have problems identifying key details—not to mention difficulty staying engaged. In fact, students generally don't see a purpose for school reading. It's up to us to have a compelling rationale—and name it for students—with every book we read. (I'm indebted here to the work of Bauman, 1993; and Davey, 1983 who provide the basis for some of the prompts that follow.)

Start by talking through how you naturally preview a text. Use the following prompts.

Book Selection/Previewing Prompts

Sample Prompts That Relate to Considering a Book's Content, Genre, and Readability

"The title/author/call-outs/pictures/front matter/author information/book design/text this is in/makes me think…"

"The title makes me think that this is going to be about a car race."

"The book this is in makes me think that this is going to be about science in everyday life, probably about electricity."

"The photographs make me think that this will be about really bad storms."

"The comments on the back make me think that professional football players think this book really captures the life of an NFL player."

Sample Prompts That Relate to Personal Purposes for Reading

"I really like X and this book connects to that by…"

"I am learning about/inquiring into/interested in learning about X and this text might help me by…"

"Oh, yeah, I read this author's last novel. I bet this is good too because ___."

"I need something light and funny to read, and this title and cover look fun because ___."

"I'm just learning to cook, and I can tell by the ingredients and directions that this is too advanced for me right now because ___."

"This may connect to my interest in/study of ___."

"Reading this may help me to find out whether there are any rattlesnakes in this area of the country and other things like ___."

"Reading this may help me to understand what breaks up some relationships."

"Reading this may help me to understand what it was like to be a foot soldier in the Civil War."

2. Make Predictions

As you begin reading, begin predicting what will come next. Correct and revise predictions as you gain information from the text.

Prompts for Local-Level Predictions

"I'm guessing that ___ will happen next."; "I bet that ___."; "I wonder if ___."

Examples

"I'm guessing that he will be captured by the guards looking for deserters."

"I'll bet that there are no rattlesnakes in Maine because it is too cold there."

Prompts for Global Predictions

"I think this book will be about [the general topic of …] I wonder if ___. I imagine the author believes ___. I think the tone of the book will be… [sad, happy in the end, pessimistic] about human beings ___."

Examples

"I bet the author fought in the war and that he will be against wars because of his experiences."

"I'm guessing that this book will be about why the Vikings disappeared."

"*Pobby and Dingan* will be sad because it starts with her friends being 'maybe-dead.'"

3. Connect Personally

Show how you use your own experience to help make meaning, and the ways you bring your experiences of other texts to help you understand this one. I call this "relating life to literature" or "bringing life to text." Beth Davey calls this process the "like a ___" step, when readers say to themselves, "This is like when Joey and I went fishing" or "This is just like that movie I saw called *Inception*."

I also ask students to practice the reverse operation, considering how they might apply what they are reading to their life. I call this "relating literature to life" or "text-to-life connections."

Prompts

"This is like ____."; "This reminds me of ____."; "This could help me with ____."

"This is helping me with/to think about/to make plans for ____."

Examples

"This story is like a video game I know called World of Warcraft."

"This is like the time that we went on a ferry to Nova Scotia."

"This book is organized in the same way as that one I read about reptiles, so I can expect that each picture will be followed by a description."

"This is helping me make plans for building a robot with Legos."

4. Visualize

Show how you take the sensory and physical details the author gives you and expand them in your mind's eye to create an image or a scene. As I've said, this ability to "see" what one is reading, to create accurate mental models and/or sensory-rich story worlds as one reads is crucial to engaged reading. Demonstrate how you develop and adapt images as you read, whether it's an expression on a character's face, the interaction of resistors and charges in an electrical circuit, the workings of an engine, the room the characters are in, and so on.

Prompts

"In my mind's eye,"; "I imagine,"; "I see ____."; or "I have a picture of ____."

Examples

"In my mind's eye I see a girl entering a dark room."

"I see a scientist working at his desk."

"I imagine a floor plan of the house, and I can see how it is organized with the kitchen in the back with a bay window."

"In my head I can see an electrical circuit plan. I see where these lightbulbs would go in that circuit and how the battery pushes the charges."

5. Monitor Comprehension

Demonstrate how expert readers constantly (though often subconsciously) monitor comprehension by asking, "Does this make sense?" Show that you expect what you read to make sense to you and that if it doesn't you will stop to identify this as a problem.

Prompts

"This is (not) making sense because ____." or "This is (not) what I expected because ____."

"This connects (or doesn't) to what I already read/already know because ____."

Examples

"This doesn't make sense to me because before it said there were three soldiers and now there are only two."

"This isn't what I expected because it was about electrical circuitry and now it is about something called resistors."

"This isn't making sense because my mind was drifting for the last several paragraphs, so I'll have to go back and reread ____."

"This doesn't make sense because I don't know what the word conjoin means, and it seems they're talking about that."

"This connects to what I read before about how the Vikings navigated because it shows how they kept exploring."

6. Use Fix-Up Strategies to Address Confusion and Repair Comprehension

Repairing one's confusion comes just a heartbeat after Step 5, of course. Demonstrate how you use various strategies when you can't grasp something or wish to check your understanding. Emphasize that even expert readers sometimes run into texts they have difficulty reading, or can't read. But when they do, they address these problems by

- rereading.
- reading ahead to see if that will clear things up.
- reviewing and synthesizing previous ideas from the text and relating these "chunks" of concepts to the confusing ideas.

- replacing a word or words they don't know with one(s) that they know and think would make sense in this context.
- changing their ideas or visualization of the story to match new information, i.e. you may find that how you have visualized the story or what you think the text is really about is in error, and you need to make a self-correction, radically reconceiving your ideas.
- asking someone for help.

Prompts

"Maybe I'd better ____."; "Something I could do is ____."; "Since I don't understand this word, a good strategy would be to ____." or "First I saw, but now I see ____."

"What I thought this was about no longer makes sense because ____."; "I need to revise my thinking by ____." or "Maybe I need to consider ____."

Examples

"Maybe I'd better read on for a few paragraphs to see if I can make this clearer to myself."

"I don't understand how this fits with what came before, so something I could do is reread the previous passage to see if I can make the connection."

"Since I don't understand this word, a good strategy would be to use the context and make a guess and see if that works."

"I thought this was about paying taxes, but the detail about using enough detergent doesn't make sense. Maybe I need to consider that this is about doing the laundry."

A student writes down her think-aloud on a sticky note.

The Moves Make the Reader

These general process reading moves are powerful, giving kids a way to use general processes that are basic to all reading tasks and applicable to all kinds of texts. They are particularly valuable, eye opening, and, dare I say, life changing, for our students who struggle most. One of my favorite stories is about Jon, who after hearing a classmate's think-aloud emoted, "I can't believe you do all that stuff when you read! Holy crap, I'm not doing… like nothing… compared to you." His classmate Ron, a teammate on the wrestling team, concluded a long commentary by saying, "If you don't do all that when you read, then you're not reading! It's like wrestling, man, you have to be there! You have to know the moves and make the moves! If you just sit there you'll get pinned to the mat!" Jon decided to "borrow" Ron's strategies and reading moves, and by doing so he became a more competent reader.

After engaging in his first few think-alouds, another reluctant reader implored, "Why didn't someone tell me that this is what readers do?"—his voice loud with anger. When I asked him why he was so upset, he said, "If I had known what to do, I would have done it!" Then he added, "Why didn't you tell us this before? Is it supposed to be a big secret or something?" "What bugs me," he continued, "is that it's really not so hard…. I guess I really didn't need to go through all that suffering and feeling stupid."

Think-alouds ensure that the hallmarks of engaged reading don't remain a big secret to a single child in our classrooms. Think-alouds are about making public the secret things that expert readers know and do, and about helping our struggling and striving readers to make those secret and powerful moves their very own.

CHAPTER 4

AUTHOR'S CRAFT, READER'S ROLE

Using Free-Response and Cued Think-Alouds to Show the Link Between Author and Reader

The process of learning is one of constantly outgrowing oneself and of building on one's current capacities to become something more. In several of my studies on teaching and learning, I've found that the most important resource teachers have for teaching something new is what their students already know and care about. If we don't access what students are already interested in, and already know and can do, then we have no resources available to us to use for helping them to learn anything new. I like to say that humane teaching is using what students already care about to develop new interests and passions, and using what

CCSS

Anchor Standards for Reading, 1–6
Anchor Standards for Language, 3–7

students already know and can do and bridging from this to the development of new and exciting capacities.

In this chapter we'll explore how think alouds are a great way to help teachers and students to both understand how students currently read (and to name and celebrate these existing competencies), *and* to help them see how to use their current competence as a springboard for taking on specific new reading strategies.

To undertake this venture, we will first explore the notion of a "free-response think-aloud," during which readers report out everything they are aware of doing as they read. This method is great for giving students—and you—a kind of panoramic view of their reading process. Students see how they read, share their characteristic ways of reading with classmates, recognize that others read differently from the way they do, and realize that expert readers call upon a wide variety of strategies at the same time—strategies that they may wish to appropriate and use for themselves. In sum, free-response think-alouds help students appreciate how they read, how complex expert reading can be, and to see where they might proceed next as readers.

We'll then turn to the powerful technique of "cued think-alouds." With these, you guide students to notice certain things about a text and an author's craft. You'll use these think-alouds when you want to develop students' ability to notice particular features of text and then apply particular strategies to interpret them.

Free Responses: When and How to Use Them

A free-response think-aloud is indeed free—it's a freewheeling monologue wherein a reader reports on everything she is noticing, thinking, doing, seeing, feeling, asking, connecting to and reflecting on as she reads. Instead of focusing only on general-process strategies of reading (as we did in Chapter 2), now we're interested in hearing every move a reader makes.

I like to use this kind of think-aloud with students early in the school year and then return to it a few times throughout to mark progress. Free-response think-alouds give me a quick idea of what students do, don't do—and could do next—as readers. This gives me crucial data that helps me plan my instruction. It allows me to name my students—even the struggling ones—as readers, and to name those strengths and possibilities that we can use to build on to keep improving as readers. The activity also gives my students a rich sense of reading, a big picture of all the activities readers engage in, and the joy and fun and meaning that reading can bring.

Beginning-of-Year Baseline: I like to have each of my students do a free-response think-aloud early in the year so that I can see how they read—their typical modes of response, what strategies they use and fail to use, and so on. Many of my students can report very little awareness about their reading processes early on. This is important information for me as I plan instruction for self-monitoring (see Chapter 4), and it provides a baseline against which I can measure their subsequent growth as readers. It's also a crucial challenge: we know that expert readers are aware of their reading processes and aware of many options and fix-up strategies for solving problems as they come up. One of the many fabulous powers of thinking aloud is that it requires developing this kind of metacognitive awareness.

End-of-Unit Exercise: I often like to conclude a unit or a course with a free-response think-aloud because it brings together all the processes we have studied, and demonstrates how expert readers integrate their use of multiple strategies into a rich reading of text. Having students do such a think-aloud can also serve as an excellent evaluation tool (see Chapter 7).

End-of-Year Measure of Growth: It's also great to use a free response think-aloud near the end of the year to show students how they have added to their cache of reading strategies throughout the year.

Comparisons with earlier think-alouds can be especially illuminating! In this way, thinking alouds can be a powerful way to see and celebrate student progress, offering proof of positive growth and achievement.

Chloe: Learning to Deepen the Questions

Ninth-grader Chloe's first free think-aloud of *The Incredible Journey* consisted solely of questions; she had interrogated the text, ripping into it like a homicide detective with literal questions like: Where is the story taking place? What kind of industry is there? What is John Longridge doing? Why does he have the animals with him?

When we reviewed her think-aloud, which I'd had her write in her notebook, I asked her to characterize how she had read this passage. "It's all questions," she replied. "Where did you learn to ask these kinds of questions?" I asked her. "In school," she succinctly replied. I agreed with her assessment, and it unfortunately demonstrates how school often works to impoverish students' views of reading and their use of reading strategies. Chloe was using the simplest and least useful kinds of questions, and not accidentally, those most often used at the end of chapters in a textbook.

I explained to Chloe that all her questions were literal questions, the answers to which could be found directly stated "right there" in the book. I told her these were necessary questions to ask and answer, but that authors expect their readers to go well beyond literal comprehension by asking and answering many other kinds of questions too. Asking the "right there" questions is only useful if we move on to ask inferential and reflective questions too—the importance, in fact, of the "right there" literal question is that it provides the foundation for doing much more important work.

I then introduced Chloe to Taffy Raphael's (1982) four kinds of QAR (question/ answer relationship) questions, which include the literal "right-there" questions, but also include "think-and-search" inferring questions, "author-and-me" questions that connect personal experience to the text, and "on-your-own" questions about life and the world in general, which are stimulated by the book but which aren't necessarily answered in the book. I told Chloe that to appreciate any text to its fullest, readers have to use information from their personal lives, from the world, from other texts they've read, and from the current text as they read, and that asking these different kinds of QAR questions helps readers to use these various information

Anchor Standards for Reading, 1–3, 4–6

QARs

Taffy Raphael teases apart the myriad questions good readers pose as they read into four basic categories. The goal for us as teachers is to guide students to internalize posing these questions automatically as they read, as they reflect on their reading, and as they discuss books with others.

"In the Text" Questions

"Right-There" Questions: These are factual questions for which the answer is immediately available (directly stated) in the text. e.g., [In Katherine Paterson's *The Great Gilly Hopkins*] Where does Gilly Hopkins put the bubble gum that she takes out of her mouth? How does Mrs. Ellis describe Gilly's new foster mother, Maime Trotter?

Think-and-Search Questions: These questions prompt readers to infer. A good reader poses the question to herself (thinks), and then pieces together details from several places in the text (searches) to arrive at an answer (an inference). A reader often "searches" by reviewing in her mind what she's read, but at times will literally search, rereading pages or flipping ahead to find evidence for her hunch. Sometimes readers must fill in important gaps in the text by connecting information that occurs both before and after the gap. e.g., Why does Gilly behave the way that she does? Why does Mr. Randolph think the house will now be more lively? Why does Gilly believe that her mother will come to get her?

"In Your Head" Questions

Author-and-Me Questions: These questions require readers to connect their own life experiences and beliefs with details from the text. To answer such questions the reader must have read the text, but must also go beyond the text and bring her personal lived experiences and/or world knowledge to bear. A reader must make a personal connection between textual details and events and her own personal knowledge. e.g., How would I react to Gilly if I were Trotter, or William

sources. Expert readers use self-to-text, world-to-text, and text-to-text connections constantly as they read. QARs reflect all the resources expert readers use when they read (self, world, texts, text at hand) and all the activities they engage in to make meaning (literal decoding, comprehension, inferencing and interpretation, reflection, critique, application).

I prompted Chloe to use the models I'd provided to ask a think-and-search question of *The Incredible Journey* and she did so: "Why is the dog so miserable?" "You've got it!" I cheered. "Now remember, that kind of question implies a certain action you have to take to find the answer. How do you know this is a think-and-search question?"

Ernest, or if I were living in the house with her? What does the author want me to think about Gilly's reactions to Trotter's house and to Mr. Randolph? How are my own prejudices similar or different from those of Gilly? What experiences of acceptance, rejection, or rebellion have I had that are similar or that contrast to Gilly's experiences?

On Your Own Questions: These questions are usually stirred by the events, topics, or theme of the text. However, the answer to this kind of question does not reside in the text. Rather, it comes from the reader thinking about the book's issues in a much wider context—not the world of the text, but the world. e.g., What are the causes of and solutions to prejudice? For what reasons do children go into foster care? How would it feel to be in foster care? How would it feel to move around all the time? How might foster care programs be improved?

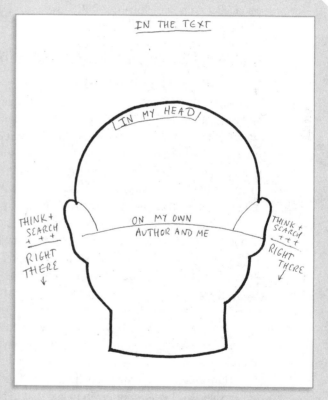

Students can use this graphic to fill in different kinds of questions about a passage as they read it.

Chloe took a deep breath. "Because I have to make an educated guess, and because the clues to why he's sad are scattered around the chapter. I have to search, think, and put things together."

"Brava!" I clapped. "You asked an inference question! Authors want you to literally comprehend what they write, but they also want you to do some work, like putting details from throughout the chapter together to build a sense of character, or to figure out a pattern or answer a question, like why the dog is miserable!"

I then prompted her to ask an "author-and-me" question, based on a couple of models, and Chloe asked, "Why does the author want me to know that the dog is miserable?"

This one-on-one work helped Chloe to build on her strength and predisposition to question as she read. I also gave her some prompts to help her visualize as she read, and had her do a visual think-aloud (see Chapter 5) so that she would develop other visualizing skills she didn't currently use.

Branwin: Learning to Read Like a Writer

Like Chloe, seventh-grader Branwin's initial free response think-aloud was overly dependent on one reading strategy. Branwin leaned heavily on making personal associations, such as "our house is painted white, too." Or "I just learned the word for 'white' in German class." She ignored key story details, including the title, if she could not find a personal association for it. I validated bringing her personal background to a text as all expert readers do, and then nudged her to go beyond personal associations, to attend to story clues with a wider array of tools, in ways that an author might expect of her and any other reader, instead of solely in her personal, idiosyncratic way.

In our conference, we talked about features of a text that authors might expect us to notice. I knew she liked to write, so I used a piece she had written as an entry point. We looked at her latest story about her cat, and I asked what she had written there that she wanted her readers to pay attention to. "The title," she said, biting her lip.

"Yes!" I responded. "Authors always expect us to notice their titles— that's even called a 'rule of notice'!"

"And… I wanted them to notice how I didn't like my cat in the beginning."

"But you never said that! So how would they know? What clues would they have to notice?"

"How I played with my dog when my dad brought the cat home," she responded.

In this way, I guided Branwin to see that in addition to noticing details that she could relate to personally, she had to be on the lookout for other details the author had selected, and she had to try to figure out what and how meaning was constructed. Just as she "coded" her own writing in certain ways, so do all authors.

Free-Response Think-Aloud: An Example

To give you a look at a teacher-modeled free-response think-aloud in action, here is the short story "The Chaser" by John Collier, along with my report out as I read it aloud. My students and I discussed this story as part of a unit about love and relationships that explores the question, "What makes and breaks relationships?"

Text	Think-Aloud
The Chaser	The title could refer to the drink you use to chase your first drink. Or maybe someone is chasing or pursuing someone. Maybe it has a double meaning? You always have to notice titles and you always have to notice double meanings—the author is sure to play on this.
Alan Austen, as nervous as a kitten, went up certain dark and creaky stairs	Check out the setting: Oh, very gothic. Everything dark and creaky. This is supposed to be scary. When you get dark and creaky you know you are in for some scares. This reminds me of those old Frankenstein movies.
in the neighborhood of Pell Street,	Am I supposed to know where Pell Street is? Is that important? Sounds like Pell Mell, like somebody is in a hurry, or like Pill, maybe this place is drug infested?
and peered about for a long time at the dim landing before he found the name he wanted written obscurely on one of the doors.	So he's never been here before and has come for a specific purpose. Why is the name so obscure? Has the person been here a long time, or maybe he does not want to be found unless someone is really looking for him and knows he's there.
He pushed open this door, as he had been told to do,	Without knocking? That's weird. So he's expected. Whenever something is weird, different, or surprising, you are supposed to figure out why.
and found himself in a tiny room, which contained no furniture but a plain kitchen table, a rocking chair, and an ordinary chair.	Pretty empty and dumpy. I can really see this in my mind—the empty room, the table and two chairs.

Text	Think-Aloud
On one of the dirty, buffcolored walls were a couple of shelves, containing in all perhaps a dozen bottles and jars.	I can see the room even better now—dirty brown walls and shelves. I'll bet these bottles and jars are important. It looks grimy though. I wonder if what is in those bottles is safe, approved by the FDA, and all that. I think NOT!
An old man sat in the rocking chair, reading a newspaper. Alan, without a word, handed him the card he had been given.	Who gave the card to him? Alan's obviously been sent here by someone.
"Sit down, Mr. Austen," said the old man very politely. "I am glad to make your acquaintance."	Very polite old geezer. He's formal—educated. That doesn't match the crummy surroundings. I wonder if he really lives here. Or this is just where he does business?
"Is it true," asked Alan, "that you have a certain mixture that has— er— quite extraordinary effects?"	Oh, we get right to the point. This is what Alan has come for. I wonder what exactly he wants and why it is so important to him. I wonder if he is an addict or something.
"My dear sir," replied the old man, "my stock in trade is not very large—I don't deal in laxatives and teething mixtures—	Yeah, you wouldn't come to some run down scary place to buy laxatives. Alan wants something you can't buy elsewhere, something sneaky and illegal.
but such as it is, it is varied. I think nothing I sell has effects which could be precisely described as "ordinary."	So he sells things that are "extraordinary." I wonder what that could be? I'll have to read on to find out!

After reading such a selection, students can identify the various cues I attended to, such as the title, the setting, the characters; and what I tried to figure out, e.g., what is the story really about, why is Alan here and what does he want; and the various strategies I used, such as predicting, asking questions, visualizing, and bringing meaning forward with me as I read. In this way, we can identify the variety of things expert readers notice and do as they read, and can identify what students are doing or might do as they read. We could also compare different readers' think-alouds of the same story and see what they might have noticed and done that I did not. This could lead to discussing what was lost and gained by making particular moves.

Prompts That Guide Students' Reflection on Free Response

You can use questions like these to stimulate discussion during reporting out, or give them to students when you want them to reflect on their think-aloud by writing reflectively about it.

- Characterize your reading of this passage, in general. How did you personally read this; what were your most popular moves? E.g. was your think-aloud primarily visual, like watching a movie? Or did you mostly ask a lot of questions, or questions of a particular kind? Or was your think-aloud transcript like an interview of the text? Did you make a lot of predictions? Did you make a lot of personal connections? Was it emotional? Or something else?

- Why do you think you read the passage in this particular way?

- What did you learn about yourself from the think-aloud? What kinds of things grabbed your attention or interested you and what does that tell about you?

- What did you learn about others in your group? How did they respond and what did you learn about them from their responses?

- What did you learn about how you read? What did you notice about how you read? About what you do and don't do? About how you compared to the other readers in your group?

- What did you learn from your group members about other ways of reading? What other strategies or ways of responding did group members use that you might want to try out?

- What did you learn about the text, how it works and what it means? What new insights or ideas about the story came up that you didn't notice when you read on your own? What did you learn from your own think-aloud? From others' think-alouds?

- What did you learn about the text topic/unit topic/inquiry question through the think-alouds? How might we use this text to think about this topic?

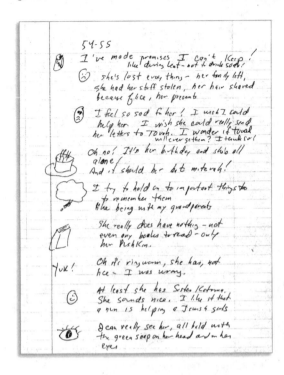

Free-response think-alouds can be used in a variety of ways, but the general point is to highlight and consider the meaning-making activity of the reader in ways that will inform future reading. This is Katlina's free response to pages 54 and 55 of *Letters from Rifka* by Karen Hesse. She coded her responses with illustrations in what is known as a "visual think-aloud."

Cued Think-Alouds: When and How to Use Them

During this same inquiry unit about relationships, I decided that I now wanted to zero in on a particular strategy that I think is central to the unit: inferring character. In fact, it's not merely a reading strategy that will help my students pursue the goals of our unit; it's a life strategy that is important to their future success and happiness as individuals. Knowing how to infer character helps us decide whom to trust, whom to hire, whom to vote for in an election, and assists us in myriad other real-life situations.

This is Katlina's free response to pages 54 and 55 of *Letters from Rifka* by Karen Hesse. She coded her responses with illustrations.

I also know that my students find inferring character somewhat challenging. (It's in their zone of proximal development.) Knowing this, I don't want to overwhelm them with all the things readers do; I want to focus my instruction solely on inferring character. Here are my most important principles for selecting a focus: it's important right now in terms of the unit and their reading, it's important for future reading and living, and it's accessible and doable.

Cued Think-Alouds:
• Coding Conflict
• Rules of Notice for Character

As I model a cued think-aloud focused on inferring character, I will cue text features that I believe the author coded into the text so that readers can infer character. The literary theorist Peter Rabinowitz calls these codings "rules of notice" (see box, page 83). There are general rules of notice, and then there are rules of notice for particular tasks (like inferring character or reading symbolism) or texts (like reading fables or lyric poems or arguments). Here we'll concentrate on general rules of notice and on special ones for reading and understanding character.

To help students notice these codes, I initially provide assistance by underlining such features and asking students to be sure to respond to all or some of these as they read. As we move along the instructional continuum, I'll ask groups of students to underline the codes during group work, and later I will have them work alone to do so.

To highlight rules of notice and how a reader is expected to interpret them, I may think aloud in front of students in the following way. Notice the underlining of significant coded text features.

Text	Think-Aloud
The Chaser	I know that titles are something we are supposed to notice. (Rule of Notice: Titles are very important to story meaning. If they refer to a character, the title is important to understanding the character or tells us to pay attention to the character.) I wonder if the Chaser is a person, like someone chasing somebody or something, or whether it refers to the drink you use to chase down another drink. If it's a character then it will be important that he is chasing something, probably something he really wants.
Alan Austen,	(Rule of Notice: Names are important, nicknames even more so.) This guy's initials are AA, like in Alcoholics Anonymous. Maybe he's a drinker and the title is about drinking. Or maybe this is just a common name for a common guy. I'll have to read more.
as nervous as a kitten,	(Rule of Notice: When a character is introduced, this is important. First impressions are the most lasting.) So I am supposed to know this guy is a "scaredy cat," ha-ha-ha. I see him as kind of wimpy.
went up certain dark and creaky stairs in the neighborhood of Pell Street, and peered about for a long time at the dim landing before he found the name he wanted written obscurely on one of the doors.	(Rule of Notice: The most important and privileged parts of a text are the beginning and the end. So I need to pay attention to what is being suggested here about this guy.) Yes, I think I am right about this being a regular guy who is kind of a wimp. I see him slowly and carefully going up the stairs, wishing he wasn't there because it is dark and creaky. I wonder why he is there anyway?
He pushed open this door, as he had been told to do,	Ah, so this is the kind of guy who does what other people tell him. He doesn't really take control of his life.

Text	Think-Aloud
and found himself in <u>a tiny room,</u> <u>which contained no furniture but</u> <u>a plain kitchen table, a rocking</u> <u>chair, and an ordinary chair.</u> On one of the dirty, buff-colored walls were a couple of shelves, containing in all perhaps a dozen bottles and jars.	(Rule of Notice: A character's surroundings reveal character.) This place is a dive. There's hardly anything in it. I wonder if this guy lives here or uses it as an office. The rocking chair is for him because he waits around for people. The other chair is for people like Alan who visit him. This guy must be a slum landlord or something.
An old man sat in the rocking chair, reading a newspaper. Alan, without a word, handed him the card he had been given. <u>"Sit</u> <u>down, Mr. Austen," said the old</u> <u>man very politely. "I am glad to</u> <u>make your acquaintance."</u>	(Rule of Notice: Any time something is surprising, or there is a sudden change, pay attention.) I am surprised at this guy's politeness. It doesn't seem to fit the crummy surroundings at all. Makes me wonder why he is here in a place where someone refined seems so out of place.
<u>"Is it true," asked Alan, "that you</u> <u>have a certain mixture that has—</u> <u>er—quite extraordinary effects?"</u>	(Rule of Notice: When a character speaks for the first time, pay attention. The way a character talks, what they talk about, the words they use, etc. all help reveal character.) Alan is beside himself with urgency. He can't wait to get to the point. But he can't spit out what the mixture is for... Is it poison? Is it magical? What does he want with it?
"My dear sir," replied the old man, "my stock in trade is not very large—I don't deal in laxatives and teething mixtures— but such as it is, it is varied. <u>I think</u> <u>nothing I sell has effects which</u> <u>could be precisely described as</u> <u>'ordinary'."</u>	(Rule of Notice: When something surprising or out of the ordinary or unexpected happens, pay attention! Anytime expectations are ruptured, look for an explanation. If it happens to a character, we are getting to see something special and important about them.) The old coot is playing coy. I bet he knows what Alan is talking about; after all, someone referred Alan to him. But he's not telling Alan what he wants to know, except that everything he sells is extraordinary. It's kind of surprising to me that this guy sells extraordinary stuff in such shabby surroundings. I wonder what's up. Something shady is going on. This Alan has passed into the criminal underworld because he wants something so bad, I'll bet.

After such an activity, we would reflect on and name the kinds of things we need to notice when we infer character. We could come up with a list like this, and put it on an anchor chart:

Rules of Notice

General Rules of Notice

Remember to notice and interpret the meaning of the following:

Titles	**Point of View**
Beginnings	**Repetition**
Climaxes/Key Details	**Surprises and Ruptures**
Extended Descriptions	**Endings**
Changes, e.g., in Direction, Setting,	

Cued Think-Aloud:
Rules of Notice
for Character

Anchor Standards
for Reading, 1–6

Rules of Notice for Character

Titles: Pay attention to titles! Does this title tell us who to pay attention to or something we should know about a character or what will happen to her?

Names and Nicknames: The names and particularly the nicknames of characters are almost always important and reveal something about the characters.

Introductions: Pay attention when characters are introduced!

Problems: Pay attention to any problem the character might have or a challenge they are facing.

Actions: Typical activities as well as actions they take and decisions they make reveal character.

Physical Description: Physical features and how they are described.

Clothing: What they wear, styles.

Way they talk/language they use: Dialects, tone, correctness, language used.

Typical setting or surroundings: Where do they hang out, how do they decorate their room, where do they feel comfortable or uncomfortable?

Friends or people they hang with: What company do they choose to keep?

What others say about them: What do people who know the character say about him?

Tastes/likes/dislikes: What particular tastes, attitudes, feelings, beliefs, soapbox opinions or antipathies does the character express?

Character thoughts: What do we learn about the character from her private thoughts, fears, and desires?

Character changes: Changes in a character are always important! If a character changes it is for a reason and the author wants us to figure out what the reason is. This will probably have something to do with the author's generalization or theme of the story.

(inspired by the work of Peter Rabinowitz in *Before Reading*)

Cued Think-Aloud: An Example

After modeling and asking students to help identify and use cues (in this case, for inferring character), it's time for them to start using and interpreting the cues in small groups (with or without the teacher) if they need the support, or on their own if they are ready. When some fifth graders I was working with had reached this point, I conducted the following class.

"All right!" I announced to my students. "All you blue-collar scholars have just finished reading Avi's *The Fighting Ground*. Since it was only a week ago, you'll definitely remember doing a cued think-aloud of the first chapter. I cued you to pay attention to what? Robby?"

Superstudent Robby crisply replied, "To Jonathan's character—what he was like and what we thought about him." Robby's answer was so efficient that I thought he might even add a military "Sir!" to his answer and give me a salute. I've always been a dreamer because in Maine no one gets called "Sir," just "Bub" or "Hey, you!" if you're lucky.

"Excellent, Robby!" I said. "Now we are going to do a cued think-aloud of the last chapter. But as you do it, I want you to underline the character cues and respond to them. And when you are done, we are going to compare Jonathan at the beginning and the end of the book, see if he's changed, explain why or why not, and try to figure out what Avi is trying to tell us about the kind of experience Jonathan just went through and how it might affect people."

The kids all yelled "Yeah!", gave each other high-fives, and got immediately to work. Oh, no, I'm dreaming again. At any rate, I passed out photocopies of the last chapter, arranged on the left-hand side of the page so they could write their think-aloud on the right side. They did get quietly to work, but without the pregame hoopla. Oh, well. Some students who were still struggling a bit worked together under my supervision, but most of the class worked independently. Here's the very end of Robby's think-aloud effort:

Text	Think-Aloud
…Jonathan <u>understood that his father's fear had not been for himself.</u>	In the beginning J. thought his dad was a wimp, that everyone was a wimp. Now he understands his dad was afraid for him, not for himself. This is a definite change because now he understands something he didn't before, and he understands why his father was afraid, because of the boy he found whose parents were dead.

And suddenly, Jonathan <u>understood more.</u>	See, he keeps seeing and understanding things he didn't because now he's actually seen the war and how bad it is. He's really changed. Well , his attitude has changed and maybe that's the most important thing.
Understood the most important thing— that <u>he had indeed been spared.</u>	See, he's thinking all this. Before, he thought people died because they weren't smart enough or couldn't shoot well enough. Now he knows he's wrong and he knows he should have died. He would have never thought all this before. He sees he's not unbeatable and that bad things can happen even if you don't deserve it.
Oh, how <u>glad he was to be there.</u>	Ha, this is a change. A day ago he was totally bored to be here. All he wanted was to go fight. He thought home was the pits!
And <u>Alive.</u>	Yeah, now he sees war is about death, not all the glory he kept talking about in Chapter 1. I just noticed that everything on this last page is about Jonathan and how he changed. I guess Mr. Avi is trying to drive a point home to us about how much you can change in one day.
<u>Oh, Alive.</u>	Yeah, yeah, yeah, Mr. Avi. I get it. The kid is really glad to be alive and he never thought about being alive or dead before.

A cued think-aloud draws the students' attention to the author's important codings, to all the inner thoughts, details, and seemingly unimportant asides that, if missed, can thwart comprehension and dampen one's engagement with a book. Through the think-aloud, the student is required to "slow his speed" and respond to all these textual cues.

In this case, my students were experienced in identifying and responding to character cues, so I asked them to identify these cues on their own and then respond. It's interesting that Robby recognizes that the whole last page is a series of cues about Jonathan's changed character. He even directly addresses "Mr. Avi" and how he as the author is making his point! (An author-and-me kind of response.)

This activity was a great lead-in to a whole-class discussion about how and why Jonathan had changed and how this helped express the point or theme of the book. Doing the think-aloud, sharing them with each other, the class discussion, and a final writing activity about Jonathan's character change were all completed during one 40-minute period.

Since the class was working on argumentation (see Chapter 6), I used the text-specific processes of argument to frame their response and then had them code their claim, evidence, and explanations after they had written their piece.

A Student's Think-Aloud–Based Written Response

At the beginning of the book Jonathan's highest value was feeling alive and at the end this value had not changed, it was still feeling alive. What had changed was what made him feel alive. This was totally different, as will be revealed! (Claim) The great Robby-ini will reveal all to those with the intelligence to understand!

In the beginning, Jonathan needed adventure to feel alive. He was tired of the same old things, of working on the farm. He wanted adventure. He wanted to fight in the war. He wanted something bigger and more important than just farming. All this evidence is in the first few chapters. (Evidence) This shows he felt he wasn't as alive as he could be and he wanted to be more alive, more on the edge, taking more risks, getting more from life. (Explanation)

At the end of the book he has totally had it with the war, people being killed, people being stupid, being hungry and cold. When he finally gets home it says "How glad he was to be there" so his attitude has totally changed about the farm and his family. Then it says, "And alive. Oh, Alive." (Evidence) You see he's glad to be home because it is safe. And he can live there without being killed or afraid of being killed. He realizes that this is what life is all about, not about extreme sports and all that and risking your life all the time. (Explanation) So his highest value is the same, but what makes him feel alive is different. In the beginning he wants action; at the end he wants to be the same, safe, and be with his family who loves him. (More explanation) So what makes him feel alive is different from being in the battle.

Cues to Conflict

Cued Think-Aloud:
Coding Conflict Types

In our reading camp, students were helped through the use of think-alouds to identify the cues of conflict (emotionally charged words, descriptions of emotions, danger, or hints of impending danger, high stakes: big costs or benefits tied to different resolutions, high stakes: something important is up in the air for a character, group, culture, or the environment), as well as cues to notice the type of conflict (for interpersonal or self vs. self conflict: the emotion is inward, character is confused or struggling with an emotion or idea or decision, there is danger but often to character's identity or self-worth, the consequences will be directed mostly at the character versus others). On our dvd, see how students were helped to code conflict types through thinking aloud in a small group.

More Think-Aloud Scaffolding for Particular Strategy Use

Students Do/Teacher Helps

Anchor Standards
for Reading, 4–6

"Say Something" Game for Pairs and Small Groups

If, after modeling and discussion, my students still have difficulty interpreting the underlined features of a cued think-aloud, I might ask them to play a version of "Say Something" (a game I learned from my friend Kylene Beers) that gives them practice summarizing.

To compose a summary, readers must notice key details (codes the author definitely wants them to notice), interpret their meaning, and string these details and their meanings together into a coherent whole. The game itself is a teacher-sponsored kind of scaffolding, and as the students' work is articulated, I have the chance to intervene and assist them.

To begin, I have students work in pairs or small groups. I give them all the same passage of text from a book or novel we are reading, and one student reads the passage aloud. Then another student in that group has to "say something" that comes to mind, and then the first student or another student chimes in.

At first, students tend to make statements about anything at all. But as they become proficient, I ask them to say something that cites a key detail and how they interpret that detail. Group members can record these statements and then link them together to compose a summary of the complete passage. Ultimately, all the key details should have been articulated so that the summary is complete. It's important that everyone in the group collaborate to decide what all the key details mean in terms of a main idea or author's generalization.

It's important to note that students may need help identifying topics and key details and how these contribute to story meaning and an author's generalization. (See Chapter 6 for more on this task-specific process.)

"Say Something Specific:" Underline Text for Greater Scaffolding

For students who still need to be prompted to notice the appropriate cues for the strategy and interpretive operations being studied, I've developed another version of the game in which students say something in response to cues I've underlined in the text. Working in groups, students say aloud what they were doing and thinking when they read the underlined textual cues. Each group member says something for each cue, and the order in which they do so can revolve with each cue. Everyone has to "say something" when it is their turn. Even if they weren't doing or thinking anything, they are cued to try to come up with something. Anything will do, even "I wasn't doing anything." As group members share responses, they are teaching each other how to deal with the cues authors leave them as they use particular meaning-making strategies. This version of the game can also involve summarizing and then basing an authorial generalization on the summary, as shown below. In this transcript, students are playing "Say Something" with underlined codes for inferring character from the end of "The Chaser." Using underlined codes keeps students focused on the task or text-specific process being studied, and insures that they are directed to report out about these particular processes. In this case, Joe is playing the role of secretary who records and will report on his group's think-aloud.

Of course, it is also possible to play this game with a specific focus on any text convention or feature present in a text: "Say something about character" worked for my class when I was teaching about inferring character, or "say something about symbols" works if a text is filled with symbolism, etc.

Text	Think-Aloud
"She will care intensely. <u>You'll be her sole interest in life.</u>"	**Anna:** YUK. It's not her who will care about him, it's some drugged-up dope. It's just the love potion that will make her love him. She won't be herself. This is what kills me. He wants to drug her up so he can be loved, not so she can love him or he can love her. What a jerk!!!
	Joe: Yeah, right. What she said.
	Tish: Say something of your own, Joe! It's the rule!
	Joe: Uh, I don't think it's so bad for him [Alan] to be her sole interest. The old guy doesn't think so either... he's using that to sell the stuff.
	Anna: You are so screwed up!
	Joe: If girls paid a little more attention to guys then we... I mean he... wouldn't be in this position. We're nice to you ladies and what do we get in return??
	Tish: You are so yuk-luk!
	Joe: Okay, you say something.
	Tish: Anna's right. This Alan schmo is only looking out for himself. That's why he listens to a sexist pig like the Old Man. They see women as things to own.... No, they see them as pets and you have to train your pets to behave like you want. That's why he says this and that's what the author wants us to see—they are both sexist pigs.
	Joe: Enough already!
	Tish: What are the key details to remember from this section?
	Anna: The potion will make her completely change and think only about Alan.
	Joe: I think we ought to include that she'll be jealous.
	Anna: When I said she completely changes, that covers that.
	Joe: (mumbles)
	Tish: Write it down, Joe, you are the secretary!

[Story reading and Say Something continues to the story's conclusion.]

Two students work together as they read and play "Say Something."

Bringing It All Together: Whole-Class Reporting Out

When students have finished small group spoken think-alouds, such as the ones students did for "The Chaser," I often ask them to report out to the larger group what they have learned. This can be done quite quickly, and it often leads to rich discussion of strategy use, the text, or the topic of study.

For example, after we did a "Say Something" for "The Chaser," students wrote what they learned about inferring character and about the story through their think-aloud discussions. The next day we reported out, recorded insights on the overhead, and still had time to do some drama activities inspired by the story. When reporting out, questions and concerns are often voiced; new insights and developing strategies are often shared. I might use prompts to guide the reporting out.

Again, structuring this kind of reflection into collaborative lessons helps students consolidate their learning and move ever closer to applying it to new situations. Our ultimate goal, of course, is for students to independently evaluate and adapt their own reading procedures. The reading process must be adapted in specific ways when engaged in task- or text-specific processes. I'll explore how to direct students to use and report out on several of these kinds of specific processes in much greater detail in Chapter 6. And of course, being able to self-report their strategy use enables students to self-assess and self-correct their reading in ways which are central to any reading process. Reporting out in this way gives students guided practice in this kind of self-assessment (for more on Self-Assessment, see Chapter 7).

Supporting Students Before, During, and After Reading

It's vital to embed your think-alouds within an instructional framework designed to assist readers before, during, and after reading a text. Think-alouds are one tool of many you will use; others include frontloading all reading, using drama scenarios, written reflections, key questions, and so on at all phases of reading where students need assistance. Think-alouds can be combined nicely with these other kinds of activities. Taken together, these practices can be integrated into what is called a directed reading and thinking activity (Stauffer, 1980). Following is a blueprint to help you build your own DRTAs, then an example of a DRTA I created for "The Chaser."

Guidelines for Creating a Directed Reading and Thinking Activity (DRTA)

(adapted from Wilhelm, Baker and Dube, 2001)

I. Before Teaching: Set Your Teaching Purposes

Set goals for your unit (or for a text you have chosen).

- Affective/attitudinal goal: What emotions and attitudes do I want to cultivate in my students?

- Conceptual goal: What content or substance do I want my students to attend to and remember?

- Procedural goal: How am I helping students to know how to do something new as readers? What textual codes am I helping them to notice, and what interpretive strategies am I helping them to use?

Effective Practices: Choose an appropriate text that is short and serves your teaching purposes. Focus on transferable goals that students can put to use immediately in new situations.

2. Before Reading: Motivate Your Students

Front-load to activate students' background knowledge and awaken personal connections.

- Purpose: What purpose might reading this text serve? How can I help students to adopt a personally relevant purpose?

- Personal connection: How can I connect students' interests, experiences, and needs to the text?

- Activate background knowledge: How can I activate personal background information and experiences that will be useful during reading?

- Build background knowledge: How can I build knowledge for students of important contexts, concepts, procedures, and vocabulary necessary to successfully comprehend this text?

Effective practices: Identifying topic of selection, brainstorming background knowledge, opinionaires, K-W-L, scenario rankings, drama, background research, etc. (For a full discussion of various motivational and frontloading techniques, please see *Strategic Reading*, 2001, Wilhelm, et. al.)

3. Beginning to Read: Preview, Set Purposes, and Enter the Text

Support student entry into the text and the reading process.

- Preview entire text: How can I help students get a sense of the text's overall structure and/or genre?

- Read first section: How can I assist students to get into the text by reading together or in small groups?

- Making meaning: How can I help students to summarize important information and text cues and carry these forward as they read?

- Predicting: How can I help students make predictions about future action that will help motivate and drive their reading?

- Knowing purposes: How can I encourage students to reflect on their personal (and academic/inquiry) purposes for this reading?

- Making personal connections: How can I help students to associate the text with their own lives and experiences throughout their reading of the text?

Effective practices: Brainstorming/round table discussion to identify class inquiry purpose, and individual reading purposes; look ahead to how text will be used after reading; teacher-modeled think-aloud, proceeding to whole-class, or small-group think-alouds; Say Something, drama strategies such as role-play, journal writing.

4. During Reading: Encourage a Deeper and Fuller Experience of the Text

Guide the reading.

- Navigating students' journey through the text: How can I cue, guide, and support students to notice key details, stated and implied relationships, structural demands, and textual conventions that are important to the strategies I am teaching them?
- Sustaining personal connections: How can I help them continue to make and reflect on their personal associations?
- Making text-to-world connections: How can I help them to engage with and learn content from the text that is important to our purposes?

Effective practices: Cued think-alouds, (sometimes cue text differently for different groups of students at different levels of ability); structured questions; drama strategies.

5. After Reading: Reflect on the Textual Experience

Take students back into the text.

- How can I help students reenter the text and reflect upon it alone and together?
- How can I help students to reflect on the constructedness and meaning of the text and reading experience?

Effective practices: Group think-alouds and reporting out; written reflections and process analyses of their think-aloud and/or the content of the book; debates, discussions of themes, drama activities, reflective, or analytical journal writing.

6. Follow-Up: Extend Understanding

Give a final assignment to synthesize a coherent view of the text as a whole and consider thematic generalizations that go beyond the text.

- Student inquiry projects or writing to encourage further connections, motivate further inquiry, and go beyond the known to what may be unknown.
- Explore textual implications of "So What?" How can we use what we have learned or decided in our own life? How might what we have learned come into play in the future?

Effective practices: Design projects such as hypermedia or video documentaries, museum exhibits, drama activities like trial of character or conversation with author, explore "What If?" situations, elaborate on text, sequel writing, set goals for further inquiry.

DRTA for "The Chaser"

1. Set Teaching Goals

- to help students personally connect to the text, bringing their life experiences to the reading and taking the reading back to their life.
- to explore our unit theme of "What makes a good relationship?"
- to use character clues to understand characters and their contribution to story meaning.

2. Frontloading: Activating Background; Building Personal Connections

- Drama scenario*: You've heard that there is a new pheromone-based perfume available on the black market. If you wear it around someone for an extended period and you are alone with them, they will begin to become delirious and think they are in love with you. You know you can get some of this stuff. What would you do? Role-play a discussion you are having with your best friend about the costs and benefits of buying and using such a perfume for your upcoming date with someone you really like but who isn't really returning your affection. (To rehearse students for the story and help them to achieve story entry.)

*My thanks to Michael Smith for the drama ideas.

- How does someone act who is like a "kitten," who is "indifferent," who says "dear sir"? (Rule of notice: Pay attention to how people are introduced, how they act and speak.)

- What adjective best describes the person you would want to spend your life with? Do they have to be this way naturally, or would it be okay if you helped to make them be this way? (Rehearse students to consider the purpose of reading the story. Is having freedom to choose part of a good relationship?)

- For writing in your journal: Think of a time you really wanted something badly. What would you have done to get this valued thing? What would you not have done? Why did you draw the line where you did? Or do you wish you had drawn the line at a different place? Why? (Prepare students to converse about the story and whether what Alan is doing is okay—according to author, and to themselves.)

3. Previewing and Purpose Setting: Helping Kids Achieve Story Entry, Appropriate Stance, Begin Meaning Construction, and Start Predicting and Hypothesizing

- Why do you think the story is called "The Chaser"? (Rule of notice: Titles are always important to story meaning.)

- Read the first five paragraphs of the story. What is your initial impression of Alan? Why do you think he is here in this apartment on Pell Street?

- Why is the old man unnamed? What do you think it is that he does?

4. Guided Reading

- Think-aloud—as you read, write down in the margins things you are thinking, feeling, seeing, doing, and connecting to.

- Respond to the underlined phrases. How do these phrases help us to understand the characters and illuminate story meaning? What kinds of things are underlined?

- As you read, try to build meaning about the following:

  - How is this story about relationships?

- What would be effective and ineffective about using the "love potion"?
- Why do you think the old man keeps talking about the "cleaning fluid" and why is this so much more expensive? How does this demonstrate new information about the old man and his potions?
- What points are being made about the theme of relationships?
- How do the characters and their relationships, and the way the potion will change these, help to make these points?

5. Discussion and Rereading

- Go through your think-aloud comments with some partners and search for repeated ideas and themes.
- Revisit guided reading questions.

6. Following Up

- Compose a personality profile of the old man for *People* magazine. State your opinion of this character and follow it with evidence from the story and what you infer from the story. What do you think about the "services" he provides?
- Drama scenario: Put Alan and Diana on the "hot seat" and interview them about their relationship before the story starts, after the love potion is administered, and then a year later. How have things changed? Prepare your answers first in small groups, then one of you will take the "hot seat" to answer questions from the rest of the class.
- What will happen between Alan and Diana after the story ends? What does this show about the nature of good relationships? Is this what the author wants us to think? Do we agree with him?

CHAPTER 5

NAVIGATING MEANING
Using Think-Alouds to Help Readers Monitor Comprehension

CCSS

Anchor Standards
for Reading, 1–6

When my daughter Jasmine and I kayak, we are constantly "reading the river" (this is the terminology kayakers and rafters use). We "read" the river because we want to know what is happening to us now and what could happen next. We need to make meaning of the river and how to navigate it. And we want to make informed decisions about what to do. We are informed in our decision-making by our past experiences on this and other rivers. When we come upon a big drop or a giant foaming hole in the river, we need a repertoire of self-correction techniques: the capacity to head upstream and "ferry" to a new position, the ability to "eddy," "scout," and "peel" out, or to find a wave to run across sideways (Bernoulli's principle for you scientists interested in fluid mechanics!) which moves you quickly to a new spot in the river, or to "boof" off of a rock. We need to know our signals so we can guide each other when the water is roaring. If things go very wrong, we need to know how to brace, roll, and immediately self-correct. Expert kayakers are always thinking of the moves they are making and will make as well as the options for alternate moves they can make if their decisions go wrong. The same is true of expert readers—they know how to make reading go well, they know how to recognize challenges, and they have a wide variety of meaning-making and self-correction strategies.

The hallmark of an expert reader, just like a kayaker, is that she actively and continually makes meaning as she reads. Whether reading a 32-page picture book or a 700-page Russian novel, an expert reader brings meanings forward as she reads each page and uses these meanings to inform her understanding of the unfolding text. She is eminently aware when her meaning-making begins to break down and has strategies to repair faltering comprehension.

Many research studies show that facility in monitoring comprehension distinguishes good readers from poor ones. Expert readers read on a global level, using individual words and local-level phrase- and sentence-meaning to construct a coherent picture of what a text is trying to express. Proficient readers are able to self-correct and fix comprehension problems as they read and have a goal in mind: understanding the larger meaning of a text and experiencing the joys and powers of that kind of comprehension.

Poorer readers, on the other hand, are often mired at the local level of comprehension as they concentrate on decoding words and sentences. They don't see how various parts of a whole text relate to each other and work together to create a larger meaning. They often have difficulty bringing the meaning of a word or sentence forward to the next sentence. Sometimes such students don't even seem to understand that reading goes beyond decoding words to making meanings with those words. And they don't see texts as parts of larger conversations—called "grand conversations" by many literacy educators—that are about important debates, issues, and intensely important human choices.

They don't understand that by reading and then accepting, adapting, or rejecting what they have learned, they have entered into the grand social conversation that is reading, not only the reading of texts, but of using texts to "read" the world.

Decoding: Words, Nothing But Words!

One of my favorite stories about this impoverished view of reading is from *You Gotta BE the Book* (Wilhelm, 1997/2008) and involves my seventh-grade student Marvin, a poor reader who could decode words. He'd spent lots of years in pull-out situations involving phonics and word-identification programs like DISTAR and the Wilson Reading Program; and these had been largely successful in helping him to decode words, but not in inspiring or helping him to become a motivated, proficient reader. I remember reading a baseball story with Marvin. I was asking him inference-level questions about things that were implied but not directly stated in the text. He became angry and said, "I am telling you what the story says. It's not fair of you to ask me what it doesn't say!" Marvin did not understand that he was supposed to bring his own knowledge of baseball to the reading act so he could create a story world and a visual image of the field, the ballplayers, and the action.

When we finished the book, I asked him what the story meant to him personally, and what the author might have been communicating about the ballplayers' actions. He was totally stumped.

"What do you mean, what does it mean? It's a story. Some stuff happened."

When I asked him what the most important events were, he told me that he couldn't remember.

Students and teacher use a "forum" or "fishbowl" to help Douglas monitor his comprehension and use fix-up strategies.

When I asked him what he had seen when he read the story, he muttered, "See? Words, man, I see nothing but words!"

I asked him to recall the point at which the story had stopped making sense. I'll never forget how sad he looked when he said, "Reading is supposed to make sense? Reading… school… it's never made any sense to me. No sense at all."

Marvin's critique of school and school reading could be interpreted on several levels, but it's clear that school had not helped him to think about reading as a meaning-making pursuit and had never helped him to view reading as a worthwhile activity. He was not aware of how to make meaning, of when meaning might be breaking down, or what to do about it when it did. He could decode most words and thought that was reading. No wonder he so often insisted that "Reading is stupid!"

If reading is reduced to constrained skills like decoding or fluency, then it is indeed stupid.

Parents and schools often collude to promote misconceptions about reading. I've had parents insist that their child could read or was a good reader because he could decode and identify words. They didn't understand that reading is so much more than that. "I don't know what the trouble is," they'd insist. Schools collude because we often teach reading, particularly with older remedial students like Marvin, by concentrating solely on word-decoding skills or on fluency instruction. These skills are very important, to be sure, but they are "constrained," learned quickly, and completed. And they tend to center on fundamental building-block information such as learning letters, names, and sounds—everyone masters the same body of information once they have mastered these skills. Phonemic awareness, math facts, prototypical features of print, fluency, and so on, stand in contrast to *unconstrained skills* like vocabulary and comprehension strategies which evolve and are infinitely transferable. Unconstrained strategies make expert readers. One unconstrained strategy set is that of metacognition, including comprehension monitoring.

Further, reading is an *integrated* process of many constrained and unconstrained word-, sentence-, and text-level strategies that help us pursue larger meanings. This kind of meaning-construction involves a variety of cognitive, emotional, personal, and social processes. Think-alouds, as I hope has been obvious thus far in this book, can highlight the many integrated features of engaged reading.

In this chapter, we'll look at ways to use think-alouds to give students powerful unconstrained strategies for monitoring comprehension and for "fixing up" their comprehension when it derails. It is absolutely essential to good reading that the reader knows when meaning breaks down and what to do about it. To do this, readers must learn to identify when problems occur, isolate the problem, name the source of confusion, and know how to use strategies to attack and overcome the confusion. This is far from a simple process, and think-alouds can be a powerful way to help develop students' capacity to master a repertoire for doing so.

Think-Alouds Can Target Common Troubles of Struggling Readers

- Poor readers often plow right through a reading, decoding words but not comprehending the text. This is often called "word calling" and was the problem my student Marvin suffered from, abetted by school and the kind of instruction he had been receiving. Think-alouds can help because they require the reader to slow down and to reflect on how they are *understanding and interpreting* text and how constrained skills like decoding are in service of unconstrained strategies like comprehension. (My thanks to Scott Paris for sharing this insight with me.)

- Poor readers don't bring meaning forward with them, building it as they work through a text. Think-alouds can help students to identify, consolidate, and summarize the growing meanings they make while reading so the meaning can be used.

- Poor readers just give up. Think-alouds can help by giving students strategies to try in lieu of giving up.

I'm indebted to the work of James Baumann and his colleagues in using think-alouds for monitoring comprehension. Their studies, among others, have shown that think-alouds are a highly effective way to help students deal with the monitoring and repair of comprehension difficulties. (See especially Baumann, 1986, 1992, 1993.)

From Modeling to Students' Independent Use: Basic Steps

Teacher Does/Students Watch

To introduce my students to the notion of checking understanding while reading, I model a wide variety of fix-up strategies, help students identify these strategies, and then post a list or flow chart of them in the classroom (see example, page 102). I tell the students that the strategies outlined here will help them monitor their comprehension and read more powerfully, no matter what they are reading.

Teacher Does/Students Help

Then I read another text and ask students to help me go through the process we have outlined by prompting me and explaining the steps I should try.

Flow Chart of Comprehension-Monitoring Behaviors

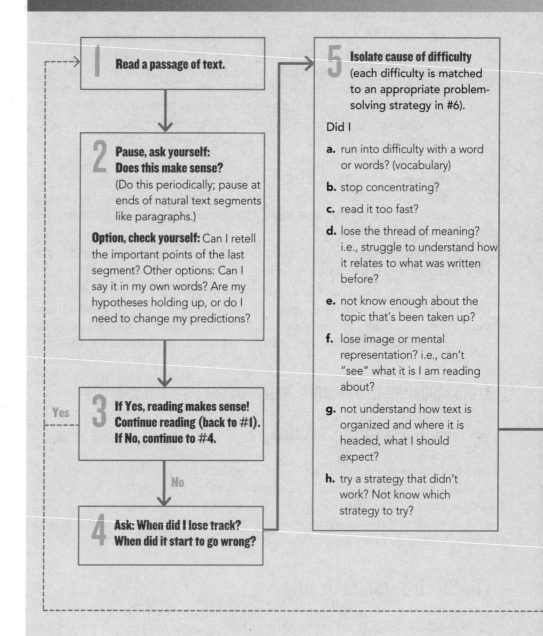

1 Read a passage of text.

2 Pause, ask yourself:
Does this make sense?
(Do this periodically; pause at ends of natural text segments like paragraphs.)

Option, check yourself: Can I retell the important points of the last segment? Other options: Can I say it in my own words? Are my hypotheses holding up, or do I need to change my predictions?

3 If Yes, reading makes sense!
Continue reading (back to #1).
If No, continue to #4.

Yes

No

4 Ask: When did I lose track?
When did it start to go wrong?

5 Isolate cause of difficulty
(each difficulty is matched to an appropriate problem-solving strategy in #6).

Did I

a. run into difficulty with a word or words? (vocabulary)

b. stop concentrating?

c. read it too fast?

d. lose the thread of meaning? i.e., struggle to understand how it relates to what was written before?

e. not know enough about the topic that's been taken up?

f. lose image or mental representation? i.e., can't "see" what it is I am reading about?

g. not understand how text is organized and where it is headed, what I should expect?

h. try a strategy that didn't work? Not know which strategy to try?

6 Use an appropriate strategy for your problem.

a. Skip the word and read to end of sentence or segment, trying to figure it out from the context.

Guess the meaning or substitute a word that seems to fit and see if it makes sense.

Ask someone the meaning of the word, look for definition in text, or look up in dictionary.

b. Reread the segment.

Read aloud—it can really help to hear the text. Or ask someone else to read it aloud to you.

c. Slow down and reread, or read aloud.

d. Chunk the confusing segment with what came before or what comes afterward. Try to understand a whole chunk that is short and manageable.

e. Identify the topic and bring personal knowledge to bear. What do you know about this or a similar topic that might help you?

Find out more about the topic—read something else that is simpler or more introductory; use a reference book; ask someone else who knows more.

f. Try to create an image or mind picture of what is going on (could use picture mapping, tableaux, or mapping techniques from next chapter).

g. Ask: How is the text organized? How should what comes before help me with my problem? (Very helpful to know that in an argument a claim is followed by evidence and evidence is usually followed by a warrant; in cause and effect text structures, causes are followed by effects; in classification, one class or category is followed by a parallel category, etc. See Chapter 6.)

Recognize and use text features and cues to text structure like transitions, headings, illustrations, captions, and charts, etc.

Ask: Am I supposed to make an inference? Fill a gap in the story? Put several pieces of information together to see a pattern?

h. Read on and see if the confusion clears up.

If still confused, try another strategy or ask for help. Ask a peer, then the teacher, or another expert reader.

Yes

7 Check understanding—if Yes, back to #1 to continue reading; if No, ask for help.

No: Ask for help.

Students Do/Teacher Helps

When the process of comprehension monitoring becomes relatively clear to them, students then take over the process themselves in small groups, and when ready, of course, begin to use the process on their own. I intervene and help only as necessary.

Tips for Guiding Students

- I start off telling students to continually pause and ask themselves the question: Does this make sense?

- I tell kids who answer "no, this isn't making sense" to use the most basic fix-up strategies of 1) rereading, 2) reading ahead, 3) skipping or filling in a word. I later introduce other strategies, some of which need to be modeled and taught more explicitly. Remember that any time you introduce a strategy and kids don't or can't use it, you must go back and do more modeling and provide more assistance. On the other hand, if kids quickly take to the strategy, let them take more responsibility for it, and move on to more complex uses of the strategy or to teach something else with which they are having more difficulty.

Students Do/Teacher Helps

The Stop, Fix, Ask Checklist

When students are ready to take over the process of self-monitoring in small groups, pairs or individually, I might give them a Stop, Fix, and Ask Checklist (see next page). This checklist is an expansion and adaptation of the Stop-Think Strategy of Sue Mowery which I discovered on the Internet and have now used for many years with my students.

Name _____ Date _____

Stop, Ask, Fix: Student Checklist

Give yourself a short self-assessment. Read through the following list and put a check mark next to the strategies you regularly use to read a difficult book or piece of writing. Which ones don't you use? These should be strategies to keep in mind the next time you read something challenging. Keep this checklist at your side as you read a text. Use it to help prompt you to use the appropriate strategies available for watching and fixing your comprehension.

ASK, When reading a difficult text...

☐ I periodically stop and ask, "Does this make sense?"

☐ I express the difference between my own knowledge and beliefs and ideas expressed in text.

☐ I express awareness or lack of awareness of what the content means.

☐ I express doubt about understanding when I am unsure or when meaning is unclear.

☐ I ask "Where did I lose track?"

☐ I identify the place where I began to lose comprehension.

☐ I use fix-up strategies when I experience problems.

☐ I reread.

☐ I read on and try to clear up the confusion.

☐ I substitute words I know (and that fit the context) to replace words I don't understand to see if that works.

☐ I make mind pictures to "see" in my head what the text means.

☐ I connect what I am reading to what I have read previously in this text, and what I have read and knew before I read this text. I may ask an author-and-me question because my personal knowledge may help me figure out the meaning.

☐ I ask myself think and search/inferential questions to figure out why and how come something happened the way it did (Why did the character do this? Why did the author put this in? How is this important? Am I supposed to "think and search" or infer?).

☐ I ask for help if I have made attempts to understand but can't get it. I ask a peer and then I ask my teacher or another adult.

Students Do/Teacher Observes

Underlining and Coding to Monitor Comprehension

Inspired by John Ciardi's colored-chalk approach to analyzing poetry, a group of my student teachers adapted this technique for use with think-alouds. The basic idea, which I've also seen used widely in the National Writing Project (I learned it from Tom Fox of the Northern California Writing Project), is for students to use colored pencils, markers, and various color "codes" to record how they are comprehending various passages of the text. My student teachers gave the technique a few new, effective twists.

CHECKING COMPREHENSION

Ask students to put a check mark in the margin of a text after each paragraph.

✓   means they understand.

✓+ means they really understand it and are really interested in it.

✓- means they do not understand and that they need to go back
and use a fix-it strategy with that paragraph.

CIRCLES, SQUIGGLES, AND BOLD

In this variation, students

__ circle words they don't know ("lassoing them" so that they are kept in mind
to fix).

__ use squiggly underlining to signal confusion (i.e., meaning is wavy and
ambiguous).

__ use bold underlining for key details (bold assertion that you are sure
this is important).

COLOR NOTES

Students use colored pencils or markers to

_ underline in green (a positive, cool, let's-keep-trucking color!) if they are getting it.

_ underline in yellow (slow down! uncertainty) if they are becoming confused.

_ underline in red if they are lost (red meaning danger!). Students also record the fix-up strategies they used—or ought to use—in the margins near the red underlining.

Of course, many other variations of this kind of monitoring marking can be used! Teachers and students will invariably come up with their own color codes, and these can be made to fit the particular needs of the moment.

Let Students Know It's Okay to Ask for Assistance

Let your students know that readers should ask for help. It's so crucial that we dispel the myth that prevails among students that "smart" readers don't ever hit an obstacle in their reading or ask for assistance. In my various studies involving at-risk boys, I found that they were so eager to appear competent that they would avoid asking for help at all costs. They would rather say, like Marvin, that "reading is stupid" than lay themselves open to the charge that they might be stupid, slow, or anything less than totally competent. (Is this a variation on men's unwillingness to ask for directions when they are lost?) I make asking for help part of the way we do things—and giving help to others part of our classroom responsibility. I model asking for a hand with many things in the classroom.

I share lots of stories about how my adult book club members help each other understand difficult passages, concepts, and books. I tell them how I e-mail and call friends when I don't understand data I am collecting, or an article I am reading. I tell them that with a doctorate in reading, I still have trouble reading many things. I stress that part of what makes me an expert is that I know when, how, and who to ask for help.

Getting It Right by Getting Righted!

I just returned from a brief break from revising of this book, during which time I went whitewater kayaking with two of my friends. The water on the Souadabscook Stream was as high as I have ever seen it. The whitewater coursed and choked down the narrow creek and swamped up over the banks.

When I first saw this scene I was ready to climb back in the car. I have kayaked this stream before but it had never looked like this. At flood stage, it gave me a new challenge, one I wasn't sure I was up for.

To psych myself up, I remembered that I had several kayaking self-correction strategies. I knew how to eddy out to catch a rest and scout the river. I knew how to brace with my paddle to keep from going over. But if I rolled or was knocked over, I knew how to Eskimo roll to right myself. If I got caught on the wrong side of the river, I knew how to ferry across for a better approach.

Thus fortified, I headed downstream. It was a scary ride and I used every self-correction technique I knew. When the run was completed, I was pretty darn proud of myself. I'd approached a more challenging task than I ever had before. I had been in several tough situations—I'd even gotten caught in a "strainer," a tree submerged in the water—but with my fix-up strategies and the help of my partners, I was able to get downriver safely and had an absolutely thrilling time. Without the fix-up strategies the scene would have been grim!

This is what fix-up strategies do for any practitioner of any craft, including reading. With fix-up strategies, kids will have the confidence to undertake new challenges. And with the help of such strategies, they can comprehend and reach new reading achievements. That can and should be a real thrill for both teacher and student, something worth celebrating. After all, self-correction, like all metacognitive strategies, is an unconstrained strategy that will lead to deepened understanding, a continuously honed set of skills and the ever-evolving capacity to learn across a lifetime.

CHAPTER 6

INTENSIFIED INVOLVEMENT
Getting Visual, Emotional, and Verbal With Texts

Anchor Standards for Reading, 1–10

Every teacher knows it. There's no denying it. The primary challenge of teaching is motivation—that continuing impulse to engage and involve oneself with reading and learning. The importance of motivation and engagement cannot be underestimated.

Given this truth, it's time to consider how to use think-alouds to increase students' motivation and engagement with the text—to psych them up for reading and to hone their ability to get totally wrapped up in the prose and to reread and reflect on their reading in ways that deepen their experience and their understanding. Just as there are strategies readers use to get into a story or to check their understanding, there are certain "moves" readers make to develop a high expectation of texts and to intensify their textual involvement, their enjoyment, and understanding of texts. Three major ways of promoting engagement are to improve the ways we see or visualize a text, to improve the way we engage emotionally with it, and to improve the way that we converse with authors and "talk back" to them about their work and the ideas expressed there. These are the strategy "families" we will concern ourselves with in this chapter.

Engaged Reading

I can't remember not loving to read. I can't remember not being involved in a book. When I finish a novel, it seems as though there are always others I've started or wanted to start, waiting in the wings. One day I'm reading *Cold Mountain*, and making my way toward that place in the Blue Ridge with Inman, doing my best to avoid the Home Guard and find my way back to my love and my home. The next day I'm sailing the high seas with Jack Aubrey and Stephen Maturin of Patrick O'Brian's seagoing sagas. It's a family joke that I won't speak to anyone or pack lunches until I've read the morning newspaper. Magazines, biographies, volumes of poetry, and coffee table books strew my office and home. The Internet beckons with Web sites galore of great interest. For me, a day without reading would be like a day without eating. I recognize my own voracious appetite for reading in some of my students. But I recognize it in far too few of them and it worries me. Not only is reading a foundational learning competence— perhaps THE foundational learning competence—but reading is also a unique, enriching, and powerful way of knowing. It is a primary mode of developing imagination, and I regard imagination as essential to human creativity, empathy, identity, and meaningful living. My own passion for reading, and my acknowledgement of its importance, is what feeds my passion for motivating students to be readers.

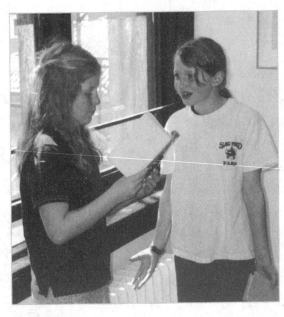

Students rehearse for a drama activity based on a novel they have just read. The activity is helping them to "think-aloud" as characters.

My reading life is filled with intensity. Just this morning I was reading Paul Hawken's *The Ecology of Commerce*. I could see in my mind the chemical companies pouring their waste into rivers. I knew that dioxin and the other chemicals they spew into the air and water do not degrade and will threaten human life for thousands of years. I argued with myself about why the environment has been lost as a theme for our current Congressional session. I became so angry about how we ignore all the evidence that we are destroying our environment that I had to stop reading. I announced, "I can't read any more of this right now." My kids, who are used to my talking aloud, looked up. Fiona asked, "What's eating you, Pappy?" But they could see from my deep breathing and distracted look that I couldn't answer right then, so they returned to their own reading.

When I read a story, I feel as though I am in that story world. Sometimes I am a character, sometimes I accompany the characters and act on their behalf—or try to. I intensely visualize characters, settings, situations, and events—so much so that I can describe places and activities that are not described, or are only hinted at, in the text itself. I often take issue with the author (especially when reading informational texts) about the way she wrote something or about the message she is trying to convey. Sometimes I actively agree or argue with her, talking back to her as I read her work, "You go, girl!" or "You gotta be kidding me!" I often choose to read a text by an author who I think I will disagree with. It fills me with the joy of engaging in a good argument.

I know from my studies of highly engaged adolescent readers that I am not unique. Expert student readers, even at the upper elementary and middle school levels, do all of these same things. Poorer readers typically do none of them. The relationship between engagement and reading achievement is at least correlative and perhaps causative. And as my own and many other researchers' work has shown (see, for example, Wilhelm 1997/2008) it is certainly the case that engaged expert reading is always informed by the affective domain.

I've found think-alouds to be one way to encourage less engaged readers to recognize and take on the attitudes and strategies that will open themselves to the intense participation and visualization involved in the best reading of stories, arguments, descriptions, and other kinds of texts. When students engage in this kind of intense experience, they begin to see why some people love reading. A whole new world of experience is opened to them. Motivation awakens and a door of possibility opens.

Visual Think-Alouds

Visualizing While Reading

Though I am aware of various kinds of visual response in the research literature, I happened to get the idea for visual think-alouds, like so many of my best teaching ideas, from my students. When I was pursuing my research on engaged and unengaged reading for *You Gotta BE the Book*, I was finding out all kinds of things about how readers enter into stories and arguments: by activating prior knowledge and knowledge of the genre, by expressing high expectations of benefiting from the text, of being enlightened or entertained, and much more. But above all, my engaged readers were quickly immersed in the text by intensely participating and visualizing and elaborating on the textual details.

One characteristic that showed up in all engaged reading was that it was a highly visual experience. As engaged readers participated in and visualized texts, without any prompting, they brought their own lives to the reading; projected themselves into the textual world; judged characters; expressed predictions and expectations; role-played and enacted scenes in their minds and even sometimes physically; referred to authors and characters as friends or acquaintances that they cared about; visualized and inferred physical features, mental images with emotional power for them, scenes and events—and much more. As they did so, they called upon a wide variety of mental and emotional processes to awaken these imaginative, intuitive responses. My data demonstrated that if students did not visualize and participate in a textual world, they were then unable to do all of the other kinds of things expert readers often do with text during or after their reading. For instance, students are often asked to reflect on their reading to consider its meaning and how that meaning was constructed and communicated through the text; to isolate and appreciate the use of writerly conventions; and to bring what they had read back to their lives to apply it.

Most of my students did not visualize or participate in story worlds in any way. I realized that my students were continually asked *to reflect on experiences they had never had* and *that no one had ever helped them to have*! No wonder they were so often unsuccessful and frustrated! So I began experimenting with all kinds of interventions to support kids' visualization while they read—picture mapping, tableaux, mind movies, symbolic story representation/reading manipulatives, museum exhibits, a variety of drama-in-education strategies, and so on. (All of these are or will be explained in other books in this series.) One day, while doing a think-aloud, a student asked, "Why can't we do drawings on our think-alouds, instead of writing?"

What?

"A visual think-aloud, kind of like…" another student continued.

"Brilliant!" I replied.

"Really?" they said, not quite so sure.

Since then, I often encourage students to use drawings when doing a think-aloud. When I offer this option, well over half include drawings of some kind. Some students, typically those labeled as LD, do their entire think-aloud, or almost all of it, in pictures. As I've argued in previous books, most of these students are certainly not "learning dis-abled." They are instead "differently abled," in ways that are not typically valued by school. Many of my LD students are very visual, and when they do think-alouds that build on this strong suit, they begin to flourish, and are enabled to use their strengths to address their weaknesses. Visual think-alouds, and the other techniques offered in this chapter, promote ways of reading not often fostered in school. When students are helped to visualize and participate in textual worlds in new ways, engagement is intensified and comprehension is improved.

Stargazing

I was reading *Number the Stars*, the Newbery Medal–winning book by Lois Lowry, with a group of sixth graders. This book is set in Denmark during World War II. Annemarie's family, like many Danes, risked their own lives to protect their Jewish neighbors from the Nazi invaders. Annemarie's family, in fact, helped their friends the Rosens, including Annemarie's best friend Ellen, to escape to safety in Sweden. In the final chapter, the war is ending, and Annemarie's family anticipates the Rosens' return.

A student's visual protocol of the last chapter of *Number the Stars* by Lois Lowry. The student uses icons to visualize what is described, indexical pictures to explore meaning, and symbols to make connections to her personal life.

Visual Protocol
Last Chapter of Number the Stars

The war would end. Uncle Henrik had said that, and it was true. The war ended almost two long years later. Annemarie was twelve.

Churchbells rang all over Copenhagen, early that May evening. The Danish flag was raised everywhere. People stood in the streets and wept as they sang the national anthem of Denmark.

Annemarie stood on the balcony of the apartment with her parents and sister, and across on the other side, she could see flags and banners in almost every window. She knew that many of those apartments were empty. For nearly two years, now, neighbors had tended the plants and dusted the furniture and polished the candlesticks for the Jews who had fled. Her mother had done so for the Rosens.

"It is what friends do," Mama had said.

Now neighbors had entered each unoccupied, waiting apartment, opened a window, and hung a symbol of freedom there.

This evening, Mrs. Johansen's face was wet with tears. Kirsti, waving a small flag, sang; her blue eyes were

I asked my students to engage in a visual think-aloud of this final chapter. I asked them to read the ending and to write or draw their visual and sensory engagement with the story's conclusion. I emphasized that this was a strategy that would make them better readers and that it wasn't meant to be an art project.

Some students drew what I would call iconic pictures or rough estimations of the literal surface meaning: for instance, stick figures in Copenhagen's square waving flags or a stick-figure firing squad shooting Peter Nielsen. A few students did more elaborate, realistic sketches.

Others drew indexical pictures, images that represented a part of something bigger or suggested something related; for example, drawing a flag or a ringing church bell to signify patriotic celebration, a teardrop falling from an eye to suggest relief and an over-whelming emotion, a gravestone to indicate Peter's execution, and a menorah on an empty table to signify the Rosen's empty but maintained apartment. Other pictures were symbolic and got at a deeper meaning; for instance, the use of a peace sign with an exclamation mark to show that peace had come to the country quite suddenly. All of these drawings helped the students to "see" and share the story world, to experience it on the levels of action and surface meaning. Other kinds of drawings, like the symbolic or indexical ones, helped students to reflect on how the text was constructed, what it meant, and how it affected them. A few students drew pictures of themselves reading and making particular moves as readers, drawing on their experience with metacognition.

Giving Visual Thinking a Voice: Discussing Students' Images

Like most of the think-alouds we do, I always ask students to share their visual think-alouds with each other and to talk about why they drew the pictures the way they did, what the drawings mean, and what they learned about the text and their reading from drawing and thinking about the visuals. The drawings always reveal more about a reader's thinking and response than is immediately obvious. Also, the pictures are objects to think with, and talking about them brings new realizations to the forefront. Neo-Vygotskians believe that learning "floats on a sea of talk" and that we must get students to talk through their content understandings and thinking processes. Visual think-alouds are great because the students have something they have made to talk about and think with.

For example, while completing a think-aloud of the last chapter of *Number the Stars*, Julieanne drew Annemarie's opened blue trunk, inside of which was a faded yellow dress topped by Ellen's broken necklace chain and Star of David. Though this appeared to be simply an iconic rendition of concrete description from the text, this student explained her picture symbolically to her reading group:

Drawing this made me see that the people had to hide themselves and who they really were to survive. And even though this is a happy day and they can come out of hiding—this is why Annemarie opens the trunk—the trunk is blue for sadness, but the dress is yellow for happy times... The dress, which is like the happy times and celebrations, is faded and worn... it stands for them and their state of mind... They are happy but they are damaged too and I have to ask if they will ever be as happy as they were before... And Ellen's connections to others, which is the necklace, is broken. It can be fixed, like Papa says, but it won't be the same. This all shows that even though they protected what they loved, the war still damaged their lives and their lives will never be the same. But the Star of David still gleams gold ... so her faith and Ellen's Jewishness are strong as ever, which is a really good sign! So I felt the great happiness of the characters and their relief, I felt glad that they still had faith, but I also felt sad to remember the people who were killed, and the suffering, which will never be forgotten. The war will always be with them.

The last drawing of her think-aloud was a two-faced figure smiling on one side and crying on the other: "This is me... totally happy and totally sad at the same time. Not confused, but both at the same time as I read the end of the book."

Though I had read the book several times, I had never seen the trunk and its contents as a symbol. This student told me that drawing during the think-aloud had helped her "to notice the trunk." "I knew it was important, and as I drew it, I understood what the author wanted me to make of it," she said.

Julieanne's incisive reading was an exception rather than a rule. Nevertheless, she was able to use the think-aloud to share her way of reading symbolic details with the rest of the class. This in turn makes her strategies visible and available to other students, who (in this case and many others I've observed) were very eager to borrow and use a more expert reader's techniques. It also gave us the opportunity to talk about symbolism and strategies used to notice and interpret a symbol. Julieanne told us that the trunk and necklace "got a lot of attention" and they "were the last objects described in the book, so I knew the author wanted me to notice them." Julieanne knew that "colors are a tip-off" too, and can be interpreted symbolically, and so are "objects people care about or use a lot, like the Star of David... or the necklace, which is a circle, and shapes can be important too!"

When she discussed the symbolism of color, someone asked whether the Swedish flag was yellow and blue. After ascertaining that this was the case, this student maintained that the trunk was symbolic of Sweden, where Ellen's family went into hiding. From this discussion we were able to put together a heuristic, or problem-solving guide, for reading symbolism.

A Reminder: It's a Means to an End

As we've seen, doing think-alouds and creating class-generated lists and anchor charts like the symbolism one just shown, invite us to calm our reading and responding pace enough that we can notice a book's crucial details and conventions and make meaning of them. It's like that old advice, "stop and smell the flowers." Eventually, readers internalize the ability to do this without slowing down to write down their comments, glance at a list, or draw what they are visualizing. The visual think-aloud has then

Anchor Standards
for Reading, I, 3, 4

The Process of Reading Symbolism: Steps to Take

Recognize Action or Object as Symbolic

Rules of notice to watch for as you read

- If an object has obvious symbolic meanings, pay attention! (For example, a menorah symbolizes Jewishness, a cross symbolizes Christianity, and a flag symbolizes a country or patriotism.)

- If an action is described in detail or seems to you to be symbolic, pay attention! (For example, if an author devotes a paragraph at the opening of a chapter to describing a wishing well outside the main character's home, he probably intends it as symbolic; references to flying often means a desire to get away or escape; names of characters and places are often symbolic.)

A familiar object or action may be a symbol if

- it relates to the title.

- it is described in great detail, or with a striking metaphor.

- the author uses the object or action in unexpected ways.

- it is given undue attention.

- a character(s) associates the object with someone or something.

- a character(s) interacts with the object.

- it keeps coming up: there is repetition using the object or action.

- characters talk about it or pay attention to it.

- it appears at an important point in the story (in the beginning, at chapter's end, at the climax, the ending).

- it appears as a surprising and inconsistent detail, or at a change in the text.

- it uses color, a number, a shape, an animal.

- the object or action itself changes in some obvious way, or is used in some new or obvious way.

served its purpose as a device for helping the learner to internalize and automatize a new strategy or strategy set.

On the next page you'll find a checksheet for students. Have them complete it after they have done a think-aloud to assess how well they have visualized. You could also use it as an informal assessment or formative assessment for figuring out what to teach next about visualizing.

2 Entertain Ideas About the Object or Action's Symbolic Meaning by Making a Cultural Connection

For example, if a text uses color, a number, a shape, you'll have to consider the *cultural* significance of the color, number, or shape, e.g., in our culture. Red usually means love, 13 means bad luck, and a circle means wholeness and harmony. Some more examples: a mirror might symbolize self-reflection; an object belonging to a deceased relative might symbolize a character's feelings about family or identity; an owl might signify wisdom; and an egg fertility, rebirth or perfection.

3 Insert the Symbolic Value Into the Text in a Way That Makes Sense, and Infer Larger Meanings That Contribute Significantly to the Story.

Now ask yourself, okay, so what does this symbol (of luck, loss, courage, etc.) express about a character? About the story's theme? For example, it's not enough to decide that the green light at the end of the dock in F. Scott Fitzgerald's The Great Gatsby is symbolic of Jay Gatsby's social aspirations, you have to infer that it represents the futility and tragedy of Gatsby's quest because he will never attain the status he desires. And perhaps, it represents Fitzgerald's own jaded view of society.

Name _____ Date _____

Visualization Checksheet for Readers

Check the moves you typically make or the moves you made in a recent think-aloud.
Provide examples. Which moves do you not make but think you could?
Set a goal to try one or two of these during your next reading.

☐ I use sensory images like sounds, physical sensations, smells, touch,
and emotions described in the story to help me picture the story.

As I read I create pictures in my mind of

☐ events and actions.

☐ characters and their features, clothing, etc.

☐ settings and situations.

☐ I create images that elaborate on or embellish story details.

☐ I may visualize unmentioned scenes or actions or details, e.g. picturing
characters when they were younger or older, seeing a setting in greater detail
than it is described, etc.

☐ I may visualize myself in the scene.

☐ I may imagine meeting a character, having the character enter my daily life.

☐ I feel emotions and may visualize in ways that heighten these emotions.

☐ I use images and experiences from own life to help me see and experience
the text.

Conversing With the Author

CCSS

Anchor Standards
for Reading, 4–9

In the schools where I've taught, we often promote the author as a mythic figure that we bow down before, and we see "uncovering" the author's meaning as the holy grail of interpretation, the be-all and end-all of reading activity. I've been persuaded by the work of Peter Rabinowitz and Michael Smith (1998) that this kind of interpretation is essential, but that it is the beginning, not the end, of useful conversation and interpretation. Rabinowitz and Smith argue that our first job as readers, just as it is in personal conversation, is to try to understand the author (or speaker) on her own terms. In other words, we read their text (or conversation) the way they want us to read it, by honoring the codes, conventions, and vocabulary that they use, and by trying to understand their text the way it invites us to understand it. Only once we have done this, which is a necessary step to respecting authors (or speakers) and granting them ethical consideration, should we then ask, "How do I feel about that message?" As we do this, we should converse with the author, and accept, adapt, or reject their meaning. I'm convinced that this kind of conversation, versus passive acceptance of another supposedly superior person's viewpoint, is essential to democracy. My middle school and high school students, particularly my more reluctant or resistant students, find this kind of work fun and satisfying. They have a natural desire to define themselves against or with others. I exploit this tendency by helping them see that authors are not all-knowing gods and that what authors write may not be well constructed, entirely correct, or worthy of their acceptance. I tell them that it is their job as readers to question, accept, resist, or elaborate upon the author's

Conversing, agreeing, arguing, and even resisting the visions and ideas of authors is essential to good reading and democratic work, both in and outside the classroom.

ideas. Since we do most of our reading as part of inquiry around important themes, my students usually have plenty about which to converse with authors.

Conversing, agreeing, arguing, and even resisting the visions and ideas of authors is essential to good reading and democratic work, both in and outside the classroom.

Teacher Does/Students Help

Drama: Conversing With the Author

The most immediate and simplest way to introduce the idea of conversing with an author about her ideas and how she wrote and constructed a text is through drama. I usually introduce authorial conversations by playing the role of the author myself (a technique called "teacher in role", see *Action Strategies for Deepening Comprehension,* second edition, Wilhelm, 2003/2012). This is a good way to introduce this kind of role-play because I usually know or can find out more about an author than my students. My playing of the author's role also models ways in which it can be done so that students will have an easier time of playing the role of author later on. My daughter Jasmine, when she was in third grade, was in a reading group that read the books *A Series of Unfortunate Events* by Lemony Snicket. (I am not making this up and the books are hilarious!) The stories revolve around compelling events and issues that almost get resolved… but then get screwed up again at the last moment. The girls in Jasmine's group often groaned or yelled when such plot twists occur. One day, they vociferously complained and moaned about the final such twist in Book One, in which the evil Count Olaf, on the verge of being arrested for his treachery, gets away when the theater lights go out. So I asked them, "Why do you think the author wrote the story that way?" and suggested that I become the author so they could ask me. They readily agreed. When they asked why I had let Olaf get away, I answered that I had, after all, warned them. I turned to page 156 and said, "Right here, I warned you, but you wouldn't listen to me! I wrote, and I quote, 'At this point in the story, I feel obliged to interrupt and give you one last warning. As I said at the very beginning, the book you are holding in your hands does not have a happy ending. It may appear now that Count Olaf will got to jail, but it is not so! Etc., etc., etc.!' So why are you blaming me! You decided to read on!"

"You just wrote that because you knew we would have to read to find out what happened!" Jasmine accused.

"And why do you keep warning us like that all through the book?" asked Lauren.

"Because I didn't want to put up with the kind of complaining I am hearing from you now!" I answered. "Besides, it's my book, and I like to be in it every now and then and talk to you all and let you know what you are in for in case you might not want to continue."

"Why couldn't you have let all the children [in the story] have a happy ending!?" Jasmine asked.

"Because he had more books he wanted to write so he couldn't end it," Lauren now accused.

"No, that is not it at all," I disagreed. "I want to make a point to you all about life and the dangers it has and how you overcome them. And it just wouldn't do to simplify it."

The conversation that followed was quite lengthy, involving summaries of various events, predictions about the next book, more accusations hurled at me as the author, and many chances for me to point out how I had written particular scenes, named characters, and intruded with my authorial presence into the text to achieve certain effects.

Hear the Author Speak

Anchor Standards for Reading, 1–8

This technique, which I learned from Rochelle Ramay of the National Writing Project, works especially well with short texts that have some intensity. When I use it, I often select stories with a first-person narrator.

I have kids go through three steps:

1. I have them underline sections of a text when they see a connection to their own life, so they can think-aloud how it connects and why.

2. I have them underline in a different color any section where they think they hear the author speaking to them. (When I introduce this technique, I have students underline the personal connections first and then go back to underline where they hear the author speak, typically in different colors. Kids can then explain why these lines felt like the author was speaking directly to them and compare their engagement and personal connections to these passages, seeing how they overlap—or not.)

3. I ask them to underline the best lines of the story (in yet another color), in which the author totally nails it. I ask them to consider what line/s, excerpts, descriptions, etc. speak for the story or somehow sums up or gets at the central feeling and meaning the author was trying to convey?

This technique helps kids to talk and write about what they notice and what strikes them as they read. It also helps them to begin considering the author and the text as a construction of that author.

Questioning the Author

An effective strategy for teaching students to do think-aloud-style questioning of the author while reading is QtA, short for "Questioning the Author." This technique is thoroughly explained in two excellent books about QtAs (Beck and McKeown, IRA, 1997 and Scholastic 2006). With a QtA, a reader interacts with a text's ideas to build and deepen understanding. "Our starting point," the authors explain, "is to let students know that the book's content is simply someone's ideas written down, and that this person may not have always expressed things in the clearest or easiest way

THINKING ABOUT THE AUTHOR GARY PAULSEN

This is a visual picture map of author Gary Paulsen, including ideas from his books and notions about what kind of person he is.

for readers to understand. Armed with the view of an author as a human being who is potentially fallible, students can view texts as less impersonal, authoritative, and incomprehensible." (1997, 18)

This perspective on authors dovetails nicely with Rabinowitz and Smith's view of authorial reading (for more on this, see page 119). For them, both literary and informational texts are constructions of meaning. As constructs, they are always open to interpretation, always arguable, and negotiable. This is just as true with so-called informational texts as it is with literary texts, which admit to being fictions and authorial constructions.

To use QtA, you divide a text into short segments. As is true when doing any kind of cued think-aloud, the segments you select should obviously contain information that you can use to model whatever you are spotlighting (inferring, questioning, accessing prior knowledge, use of symbols, and so on).

Beck, et. al. suggest that you use queries—prompts which are designed to assist students to grapple with the author and her ideas, as well as with the way the author has constructed the text. (They differentiate queries from teacher questions, which are generally designed to test literal understanding or start discussion.) These authors provide model queries for both narrative and for informational text. But as a way of transitioning to the informational structures in the next chapter, let's focus on the informational queries here. It's important to note that I have used their queries as models for my own adaptations.

QtA for Informational Texts

Start-Off Queries

(also known as Initiating Queries/Global Queries)

Anchor Standards for Reading, 1–5, esp. 6

    a. Who is the author of this piece? What do we know about this author?

    b. What might be her purpose and agenda in writing this text?

    c. What is the author writing about? (What is the general topic or issue?)

    d. What important information does the author present? (What are the key details?)

    e. What is the author's point? (What is the main idea or central focus? What conclusion do the key details add up to?) What does the author want me to know, think, believe, or do?

Follow-Up Queries

(also known as Local-Level Queries)

    a. Who is the audience for this piece? (Am I part of this audience? What would I have to know, believe, or be to become part of this audience?)

    b. What does the author want this audience to know?

    c. What does the author want the reader to notice in this segment? and think as a result?

    d. Why is the author telling the reader this information right now?

    e. How does this information connect to what the author has already told the reader?

    f. How is the text organized to reinforce key details and the main point the author is trying to make?

    g. How does this information and the author's point connect to what the readers already know and issues they already care about?

    h. Does the author tell the readers why we should think this way? Is the author direct or implicit about making her case?

    i. Am I convinced or unconvinced by the author? Why?

    j. How will this text inform how I think, read, and act in the future?

Guidelines for Determining an Author's Main Idea

I developed the following set of guidelines with a group of seventh graders over several weeks. The process of creating such a list of problem-solving strategies is incredibly effective, so while you should use this example to guide your thinking, you should also invite students to collaborate on one of their own.

**Reading Nonfiction
for Main Idea**

I. Identify the Topic of a Piece

To find clues to topic

   a. Look at the title.

   b. Look at the first and last paragraph—the topic is usually named.

   c. Ask yourself: What is discussed throughout the whole selection? What subject/s spreads across the whole text? (Note: Most texts have multiple topics. Sometimes there is a central topic, but more typically, several central ones.)

   d. Look at captions, pictures, words in bold, headings, and so forth for clues to topic. What do all of these have in common?

   e. Remind yourself: The topic must connect to ALL the major details and events from the selection.

   Caution: Not every detail has something to do with the topic. The topic is the common element or connection between major details.

   f. What do all major details share in common?

Check Yourself: It's Not the True Topic if...

**Anchor Standards
for Reading, 1–3,
esp. 2**

   a. It's too general or too big. (e.g., a topic statement that suggests or could include many ideas not stated in the text.)

   b. It's off the mark, totally missing the point.

   c. It's too small. It only captures one detail, rather than all of the key details.

   d. It captures only *some* of the key details, but not all of them, for example, maybe you didn't think about the ending.

Questions to Check Yourself

   a. Does the topic I've identified give an accurate picture of what the whole selection is about?

b. Was I as specific as possible while still accommodating all the key details?

c. After naming the topic, can I now specifically picture in my mind what happened or was communicated in the text? or might I picture something different? If so, how can I change my topic statement to correct the problem?

2. Identify all Details/Major Events

Authors often plant important ideas/key details in

a. the title.

b. details that reflect or refer to the title.

c. details at the beginning of a text.

d. details at the end.

e. surprises, revelations, and whenever your expectations are not met.

f. repetition.

g. lots of attention given to a detail, for instance, long explanation or description.

h. subheads and italicized text.

i. changes in character, tone, mood, setting, and plot twists.

j. a question near the beginning or the end.

Check Yourself: It's Not a Key Detail if...

a. It's interesting, but it doesn't develop the topic/lead to the central focus and main idea.

b. It remind us of something and is even personally important, but if you were to remove it from the piece, the piece wouldn't lose any significant meaning or impact.

Questions to Check Yourself

a. Are all the details related to the topic?

b. How do the key details relate to each other?

c. What pattern do they make?

d. What point do they repeat or add up to through and because of this pattern?

3. Identify the Central Focus (the Main Idea or Point the Author Makes About the Topic)

a. The statement of central focus you name must make a point about the topic and cover the whole selection.

b. Ask yourself: Is the central focus directly stated? If not, it must be inferred.

c. Which details help me decide on the central focus? Why are these details important?

d. The central focus considers how the details relate to one another or lead to one another (what caused or led to what). How did you consider the relationship and pattern between key details (e.g., the difference between the beginning and end of a story) as you considered the central focus?

e. The central focus must consider the ending and how the details or events led to this final conclusion.

Check Yourself: It's Not the Central Focus Statement if...

a. It is so literal and specific it doesn't allow the reader to apply the main idea to his own life.

b. It is too general—more like a topic statement than a main idea.

c. It is true but misses the point of the text. It wasn't what the author was talking about.

d. It misses the point.

e. It only fits one detail or event, not the whole text.

f. It does not incorporate all details and their pattern.

g. It doesn't fit and reflect the ending or final situation.

Questions to Check Yourself

a. What point do the key details repeat and add up to?

b. Is the central focus a statement about the topic?

c. Is it something useful that can help you to think or act in the world?

d. Also consider: Do you agree with the statement as applied to life? Why or why not?

Authorial Reading: Contemplating What's in an Author's Head and Heart

Researchers Rabinowitz and Smith urge us to aim high—to have our students become "authorial" readers. An authorial reader asks: What does this text mean to the audience it was written for, and how do I feel about that? Much like the kind of reading Beck et al. advocates in Questioning the Author, authorial reading is an active reading, a critical reading, and a feisty reading, if you will. Such a reader doesn't merely let a story wash over him, receiving a narrative much like a shore receives a wave, but exercises thought. He thinks about—and perhaps discusses with others—what a book's characters' seem to express about humanity, what the author meant to say about this larger world issue, and how he, the reader, feels about that. In short, these readers try to discern what the work implies about the state of humankind. What English teachers call "theme" can sometimes be pinned with one word, such as "justice"—which really refers to a topic; in contrast, an author's generalization implies propositions about the world and human beings. For example, a topic of *Don't Pat the Wombat* might be identified as relationships. The author's generalization proposes that adults who wield power disrespectfully over students will not be able to engage in fruitful relationships with them, and that the best relationships are those of mutual respect and support. The activities presented in the following sections help students converse with an author in various ways in order to become authorial readers and in so doing, attain a deeper level of comprehension, particularly regarding main ideas and author generalizations.

Backtalks

Some teachers like to use a version of think-alouds called "talking back." This technique is different from the think-alouds we've seen thus far, because students are stopped after reading a segment of text and asked to think back and report on what they noticed, thought, and did as they read. It's a reporting later instead of an as-it-happens account.

I created a variation I call "backtalk" in which students, after a segment of text that presents an argument, a piece of evidence, an interesting observation, or an opinion, converse with the author about their take on the information. They might choose to agree, disagree, keep an open mind, or add to the author's ideas. As students get better at this, I ask them to support their views on the issue with evidence from the text and beyond, as I'll explain in the Chapter 7. When kids read stories, it works well to invite them to talk back to a character about something she

Fifth graders peruse the editorial page of a local newspaper, searching for a piece that captures their interest.

has said, done, planned, or felt. Students enjoy providing alternative views or advice for the character and in the process deepen their understanding of the story. Or, as you saw in the drama example above, students can talk back to students or the teachers "in role" as characters or authors about how they have treated characters, and so on.

Talkbacks and backtalks tend to be shorter exercises than think-alouds. For example, if I'm reading aloud a novel, I might spontaneously ask kids to spend three to five minutes talking back about a particular passage in pairs or a small group. Talkbacks are guided, usually completed in response to a few prompts as in the case of the QtA. Backtalks are direct responses to a character's or author's actions and ideas. Backtalks work particularly well at the end of natural text segments, such as chapters or the end of books. Kids easily internalize the skills involved and become more adept and aware of monitoring their engagement, explaining it, and conversing with authors and ideas in "grand conversations" about ideas that affect them and the world they live in. This is an empowering and democratic move for student readers, particularly reluctant readers who may have spent many years disenfranchised by school and kept outside as nonparticipants in these very conversations.

Op-ed pieces from the newspaper work particularly well for this. So do news articles or features about volatile subjects, particularly ones that quote people who come from different perspectives. Stories where characters have questionable views and take interesting or questionable actions are good, too.

On the following page you will find a checklist that students can use to both guide their backtalks and to assess how well they are recognizing craft and conversing with the authors about that craft and the ideas expressed through it.

Name _____ Date _____

Conversing With the Author Checksheet

(✓+ for always, ✓ for sometimes, ✓- for not yet)

I, the reader

___ notice/comment on the way a text is organized or the way in which information is withheld and presented.

___ notice/comment on the words and vocabulary used.

___ notice/comment on the style of the author.

___ notice and identify conventions/textual codes used by the author.

___ notice and comment on how conventions and constructions are used to make the author's point.

___ evaluate the way the text is written.

___ indicate some conception of the author, what kind of purpose she has in writing this text, what kind of person she might be, and so on.

___ consider the author's meaning, the point being made through the text.

___ indicate agreement, adaptation to, or argument with the author's meaning.

___ indicate reason for agreement or disagreement.

___ indicate ways in which story meaning may inform my own thinking and action.

Which of these moves did you make in your latest backtalk? Give examples. Which ones did you not try but think you might like to try with your next reading?

Learning From Book Clubs

Last night, my book club discussed Nicole Krauss's *The History of Love*. It's a stunning book and we all loved it. This was a surprise as my book club is an eclectic one filled with strong personalities, and it's rare that we agree upon anything! Much of the discussion revolved around the issue of how much of what happened in the book should be construed as having really happened, and how much as imagined by the characters. Wita read aloud several sections and did a think-aloud variation tracing why these sections made her think that everything after the first few chapters had been imagined. Gemma read a section and thought aloud about how much she related to and loved the major characters and how this made her want to believe that everything that happened later in the book had actually happened to them, since she found the conclusion so moving and satisfying. She read some of the conclusion and wiped away a tear, then sniffled for a bit.

Geoff read a description of the protagonist looking at himself in the mirror. Then he reread it, laughing with enjoyment, following up with a comment about how much he loved the author's style and insights, and how well he could "see" the character looking in the mirror.

Mark then began a discussion about the author, and how she could have possibly developed such insight and sensitivity at her young age (31 at the time of publication). We talked about what life experiences and relationships, perhaps with relatives who had survived the Holocaust, could have informed her writing. Gregor, as is typical, kept interjecting: "But what does it mean?" Wita asked her standard question: "Is it literature?" Group members leaned forward to give their opinions, flipping through their copies to justify their thinking.

My book club (we often call ourselves an eating club with a reading disorder since we gather monthly for a sumptuous dinner) is a good one. Whether we like any particular book, or whether we agree, we intensely engage with characters, events, and ideas. We consider what the text means and how it was constructed to mean that. We always consider the author and think about her as a presence behind the text. Our meetings are intensely satisfying to all of us and we look forward to them immensely.

I propose that we think of our classrooms as book clubs and that, like expert engaged readers, we use variations of the think-aloud technique to enhance our students' visual, emotional, and authorial engagement with text.

CHAPTER 7

EXPLORING POSSIBILITIES
Merging Think-Aloud Techniques With Multimodalities and Technologies

On the morning I am writing this, my newspaper announces that for the first time ever more electronic books were sold in a previous month than paperback and hardcover ones. I'm assuming this is in part due to the recent release of the iPad. Still, the article impressed upon me yet again how texts are becoming increasingly electronic and multimodal. In his wonderful book *Writing Space*, classics scholar Jay David Bolter (1991) explains that literacy has always meant the capacity to use the culture's most powerful tools to create and receive meaning. Those tools are now electronic and multimodal.

Bolter also argues that superior technology always supplants older ones over time—and not too much time at that.

CCSS

Anchor Standards
for Reading, 7, 9
Anchor Standard
for Writing, 8

For those who disagree, Bolter would tell you to go to your local library and visit the scroll section. Guess what? There won't be one! For that matter, ask to see the codex section. The librarian will look at you like you are wild-eyed and crazy, a luddite, who must have asked for *bodices* because there will be no *codices!*

These text technologies were *utterly and entirely* replaced by Gutenberg's book. Likewise, Bolter argues, Gutenberg's books will be completely replaced by electronic hypertext. This does not mean that novels or poems or any other kind of genre will disappear, only that they will appear in a more usable and flexible hypertextual format.

What's the take-away for us as teachers? In short: we need to get hip to using electronic texts and teaching interventions in our classroom. I foresee the day in the not-too-distant future when all students will have some kind of electronic pad and will download texts, customized textbooks, and activities onto them. The book as it currently exists will largely disappear. Until that day arrives, we need to do what we can to use electronic texts, and likewise, to use these texts and electronic tools as we use think-alouds (and other teaching techniques)—as a teaching, sharing, and learning technique. However, a caveat: researchers like Richard Lehrer have found that most teachers tend to use new technologies in outmoded ways, e.g., as electronic worksheets, instead of powerful tools for leveraging and extending new ways of teaching and learning.

Here are just a few ideas that I have been working on lately with various teachers around the use of technology with think-alouds.

Googledocs offers many opportunities for collaborative composing, including the composing that is involved in thinking aloud. Typically, the instructor creates a document and shares her process of highlighting and commenting on it with the class for modeling or "teacher does, students watch" (Wilhelm, et al, 2001; Wilhelm, 2007), then students can help the teacher compose comments for "teacher does, students help" which moves into the mentoring phase. Students can then add to the same document in pairs or small groups for "students do, teacher helps," which is another phase of students mentoring each other. Then, students could proceed to create a think-aloud with another similar excerpt or text to share with a thinking partner, and the teacher can take a look to monitor the process through the "student does, teacher watches," intervening only as necessary.

As the teacher models and then involves the students, it is important to list cues and create an anchor chart to capture the repertoire or "heuristic" for using a particular strategy or strategy set.

Bringing Frankenstein to Life Through Think-Alouds!

Here is an example I used with *Frankenstein*, developed with my colleague Rachel Bear and shared through an NCTE Webinar (2010). This think-aloud is designed to help me both model my response and to help the class figure out and create a heuristic for how to read the particular genre of epistolary text. We used the beginning of *Frankenstein*, (the major text in our "What are the costs and benefits of technology?" inquiry unit) and we discovered that reading an epistolary exchange also involves learning to engage in attendant task-specific processes: namely inferring character and evaluating the narrator and his reliability.

**Forms/PDFs:
Cued Frankenstein
Model**

Inferring a narrator's character (and other characters that are described) and evaluating that narrator's reliability is part of the genre (or text-specific processes) of reading epistolary texts because you always have to make these moves when reading letters, diaries, and the like, but these are also task-specific processes used in many other kinds of texts, e.g., one has to infer and evaluate character in any text with a character, and judge narrator reliability in any kind of monologue, in political ads, short stories, etc., that have a first-person narrator.

I first introduce the strategies we will use and their purpose (what and why) and highlight in pink the cues students need to notice (when). They must use the cues at tip-offs to use specific strategies to construct meaning necessary to comprehending the text (how).

I then model my think-aloud, highlighting cues I think I must notice about character and narrator, then type in interpretive think-aloud comments (focused on interpreting character and judging narrator reliability, since this is a cued think-aloud) stimulated by these cues. Later I highlight new cues—similar to the ones I have already identified and modeled—for the students to attend to with me, in their small groups or pairs, and then individually. I often begin the mentoring by prompting students what to do with the highlighted or underlined cues, as will be seen below. Later they can find their own cues and compose their own responses without my prompting.

August 13th, 17—, The date tells me that this is a letter or a diary entry, so I will have to pay attention to the dates and who is writing and to whom. It's interesting that the author doesn't provide the year - perhaps to maintain some mystery or in hopes that the book won't become dated? Since this is the beginning of the text, there's going to be privileged information. We will have to pay special attention.

My affection for my guest increases every day. This sounds like a female writing. That's a primary task in reading diaries or letters—who is the writer and what kind of person is she? Tip-offs are word choice like "affection". Obviously we are supposed to be wondering who the guest is and why he is here. **He excites at once my admiration and my pity to an astonishing degree.** Admiration and Pity? This is another tip off: when things are inconsistent or oxymoronic you need to pay special attention. I am inferring that the writer is sensitive and is going to fall in love with the guest.

Complete sample available on DVD.

Here is an anchor chart of questions for evaluating narrator reliability that we created while doing our think-alouds.

Anchor Standards for Reading, 3–6

Questions to ask as you evaluate a narrator
1. Is the narrator too self-interested to be reliable?
2. Is the narrator sufficiently experienced to be reliable?
3. Is the narrator sufficiently knowledgeable to be reliable?
4. Is the narrator sufficiently moral to be reliable?
5. Is the narrator too emotional to be reliable?
6. Are the narrator's actions too inconsistent with his or her words to make him or her reliable? (see Smith, 1991, 16)

Here's another way to use Googledocs for a group think-aloud (see the DVD for a model with a poem). One student uses a text excerpt put up on Googledocs and chooses a color for highlighting (for example, red). He then highlights the text sections that he wants to respond to and clicks "new comment" to record his comment about the highlighted cues. A colored comment shows up on the side of the text, but can also be shown through a "reviewing pane" at the bottom of the text by clicking on "review pane" under "show." The next student then follows up with a first pass, too, choosing a different color (let's say blue) to record her comments.

The second think-aloud can be about the text excerpt AND the first response. The second reader can use the first think-aloud to inform her new one. This is what I call a kind of "think-together"—mirroring the cascade of a deep discussion about a text, what it means with discussion points building on each other's ideas in dialogic fashion. This can become a kind of silent group think-aloud that is in fact a "silent discussion" (Wilhelm, 2007).

Another option is for students to simply collaborate together and type one set of responses as a pair or small group. This can always the be sent on or followed up on by another group.

To designate who is responding, you can assign a color to each student or group so the teacher can track who responded—and/or have students initial their comments.

I sometimes have students write their e-mail address down on two notecards and then give their notecards to two other classmates. This designates their two thinking partners for that think-aloud activity. Each student provides a Googledoc think-aloud of a reading OR a written paper of their own to respond to. Then each student goes into Googledocs and "shares" her reading and think-aloud with the two selected peers. This works well for building a group think-aloud and with peer editing of student-written papers—each thinker or author choosing two peer editors who are given the right to read and respond to their think-aloud or paper through Googledocs.

The first thinking partner uses a red highlighter to go through the think-aloud or composition and writes a summary comment (such as a Praise-Question-Suggestion) at the bottom, also in red. The second thinking partner highlights using blue and comments in blue as well. The two peer responders sign their comments so they "own" them and the writer can respond with questions either verbally in class or send a message to the thinking partners via e-mail or Googletalk. With both thinking aloud and peer editing, the two "peer responders/editors" read through, edit, and respond to the first student's own think-aloud or writing as a kind of peer-editing think-aloud.

A follow-up option is to then have the different students analyze and reflect on their different comments for content, focus, length, how previous comments influenced their ongoing response and thinking, and so on. In this way, the kids are involved in a conversation about not only the text and their response to it, but in a metacognitive meta-conversation about how they made meaning of the text, how the various comments or discussion assisted in meaning making.

Another technique that I call "synchronous chats" involves students doing an online chat or texting to each other in real time. I break the text into sections, or give the students time limits —like 3-5 minutes— to focus their thinking aloud on specific issues or questions from each section, e.g., what the text means, how this meaning is connected to the inquiry, how it is constructed to mean what it means, or how the text makes use of certain conventions we are studying, such as elements of argument, figurative language, symbolism, or anything else.

Of course, this could be done through IM, texting, or even on a wiki or other social networking medium, too, as an asynchronous chat. But for this to count as a true think-aloud, the students need to get their processing down and share this. There are many software programs that help with this kind of work, and new programs and platforms are continually evolving. Facebook, Googletalk, Joomla, and Ning all have chatting options and Camfrog or Skype can be used for synchronous video conferencing –this can be done at home, with students from another class, a partner school, a reading buddy, pre-service teaching students, and so on. For asynchronous discussions there are some really cool online programs such as Stixy (you create a page with an excerpt of a text you want response to—from your reading or your own writing—and people can post "sticky note" comments just like you would do a sticky note think-aloud with a hard copy of a text); Youstickit.com (a student can share a text, write down notes or ideas, and friends can respond using sticky notes); phpBB (a free online discussion board, much like Blackboard); and so many more! Online collaboration is such a useful tool because kids today are more tech savvy and therefore LOVE to do anything on the computer. Several teachers with whom I work host wiki and Ning sites and use these for online collaborative think-alouds for poems—the energy, comments, and reactions are priceless. To get a flavor, check out this site: http://www.feedmyapp.com/web_20_collaboration_applications_sites. It lists a bunch of online collaboration sources, most of which are FREE!

Another idea is the electronic quote scrapbook: With Kindles and e-books or other electronic texts, students can easily cut and paste quotes they find significant as they read— and describe at the time of choosing why these quotes seem significant, answering questions such as: Why did you notice this quote? How do you connect this quote to the inquiry or to developing patterns in the text? Where do you think this quote is leading us? What do you think or feel about the quote? The sticky note applications work well with this activity. Kids can collect quotes—and notes and responses to them—over time that can then be used in culminating activities like Socratic seminars, final projects, and compositions. The quote scrapbook and think-alouds about the quotes are collected throughout a unit as fodder for these final reflective activities.

If students choose three or four quotes during a single short reading assignment, the quotes can be used to foster discussion with techniques like "Save the Last Word" or "Silent Discussion" (see Wilhelm, 2007). The simplest way of doing this is to ask students to come prepared to read a passage that made them think or that moved them in their reading, and then to explore *why* it moved them. A variant is to ask students to write the answers to three questions: (1) How did you "think through" an excerpt or powerful passage of this text? (this is a think-aloud excerpt), (2) How do you think the author was trying to change how people think and feel by what he or she wrote? (this is authorial reading, that considers the author as the constructor of a text and textual experience, see Wilhelm, 2007), and (3) How was your *own* thinking and feeling changed, in small or large ways, by what you read? (this is a "think after" excerpt). These techniques can be used in discussion groups without technology, of course, but can also be used online with the applications we've discussed here.

Multimodal Think-Alouds

It's also powerful and good fun to use multimodal think alouds (like extensions of the visual think-aloud) that combine thinking aloud with other kinds of instructional techniques and support like visualization or drama/action strategies.

A great introduction to thinking aloud is just to have kids think through or do a process analysis of a typical daily task, like programming a DVD or tying their shoe. They can incorporate visual models, photographs, and other concrete displays in their report on this. Another great introduction that can work as unit frontloading is to invite students to do a think-aloud of a multimedia text like a cartoon, photograph, YouTube video, video excerpt, painting, collage, and so on, that has something to do with the topic of the inquiry unit. For example, as frontloading for the "What Work Does Funny Do?" unit, Rachel Bear and I had students watch a Simpsons episode, completing a think-aloud in which they listed what made them laugh. Later, we used this to come up with a list of conventions for satire. We applied this heuristic to a later think-aloud of Jonathan Swift's "A Modest Proposal" on Googledocs. Whenever you do this kind of work, ask what the author or artist wants them to notice, why the reader/responder is expected to notice that, and what they as readers are to do with what they notice to make meaning. These questions will lead you well on your way to creating an applicable heuristic.

Forms/PDFs:
Modest Proposal
Satire "Text-Specific"
Think Aloud

A variation I've just begun to experiment with is to have students read along with audiobook recordings, and then to speak their think-aloud into a voice recorder. This can be turned into an audio file and added to by a peer responding to the think-aloud.

A drama-oriented technique is to have students do a think-aloud as a character who was involved in the scene the students are reading, who was not involved but would be interested in it, or as a character or author from a different text that we've already read. Another variation is to have students do Facebook updates in role—showing their thinking as a character at different points in a story.

You don't even need technology to do such work. At left, please see Becca's facebook page for Victor Frankenstein, which she did on construction paper.

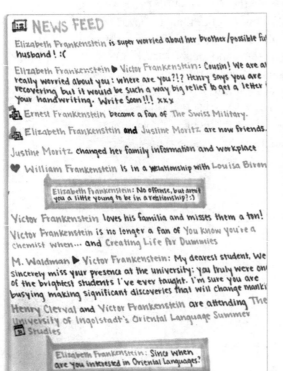

Blogging Progress

I've had students post daily blogs showing their thinking aloud as an "expert reader" of that day's reading, or posting such entries from a critical theory/reader response lens or in-role as a character from this book or another from the unit, or as an author of a different book, or a historical figure, and so on.

There are many applications that support this kind of blogging: Ning, Edublogs, Wordpress, Blogger, Bravenet, Multiply, WindowsLiveSpaces or, just go to the following site and see a bunch of them: http://mashable.com/2007/08/06/free-blog-hosts/

Another idea is to have students go in the role of the author and do an author think-aloud as they read. What was I thinking as I wrote this? Why did I write it in this way? How happy am I with it? What do I expect of the readers of my text at these particular points? What do I expect them to know and be able to do?

As you can see, the possibilities are endless. Have fun experimenting! I'd personally love to hear what you come up with! Ask your students to experiment as well and share these with you and the class. As I've said, many of my best teaching ideas come directly from my students—but only if I encourage them to share. Sharing our thinking is one of the very greatest benefits of think-alouds.

Book Notes

Teaching Text-Specific Processes

Understanding Unreliable Narrators (Smith, 1991, NCTE) offers a clear discussion of the specific expectations that ironic narratives place on readers and a practical sequence of texts and activities that can teach students how to read irony and judge unreliable narrators. This text also offers an excellent example of sequencing instruction so that students learn text-by-text and activity-by-activity, with responsibility and expertise gradually handed over to the students. See also Smith (1989) on teaching students how to read irony in poetry. George Hillocks (1995) takes a close look at the demands of fable-writing, satires, and argument-writing in his book *Teaching Writing as Reflective Practice*.

CHAPTER 8

NEW GENRES, NEW READING MOVES

Using Think-Alouds to Teach Students About Text Types and Text Features

consider a "text type" to be synonymous with "genre." I agree with literary theorists like Jonathan Culler (1972) and Peter Rabinowitz (1988) who define a genre or text type as any set of texts that share the same expectations of readers. In other words, if a reader has to notice the same codes and conventions, meet the same demands, and read two texts in the same way using the same interpretive operations, then these two texts belong to the same genre or class of text types. These theorists argue that one of the problems posed for teachers and students is that we typically construe genres too broadly. For instance, many anthologies

CCSS

Anchor Standards for Reading, 5–10

Anchor Standards for Writing, 1–4

define "poetry" as a genre. But lyric poetry, for example, uses totally different codes and structures than other kinds of poetry. To help readers, we need to slice genres more finely, into text types like lyric poetry, ironic monologues, and concrete poems—groups of texts that share characteristics and expectations.

Planning Your Genre Instruction: Tools That Help

So how do you figure out what expectations particular kinds of text types make on readers? One way is to do think-alouds with that genre to see what successful readers do and what less successful ones miss when reading a particular type of text.

Another way is to use the "inquiry square" I have adapted from the work of George Hillocks. Basically, this square (see sample, next page) is a problem-solving guide that can help you think through what is required to write (and read) a particular kind of text. It guides teachers to think through the five kinds of knowledge readers and writers must use when comprehending text.

1 **Knowledge of purpose**—knowing the purposes that can be fulfilled by the genre. Why is this genre powerful? Why do people read and write this text type? What work does it get done? This kind of knowledge is the prerequisite and the foundation of all engagement and comprehension.

2 **Procedural knowledge of substance**—knowing the process of activating or finding the background information you need, and knowing how to decode the textual cues and conventions to get after the text's meaning. This is the cornerstone of all comprehension and understanding, knowing how to get the content or "stuff" necessary for making meaning.

3 **Procedural knowledge of form**—knowing the process of using structural conventions and reformulating these in your mind so that you know how the text is constructed to create meaning and foster response.

4 **Declarative knowledge of form**—being able to name the text type, its structural components, and how these work together to create meaning. Declarative knowledge becomes conceptual when the "toolishness" of what is named is understood and can be used in one's future reading and composing.

5 **Declarative knowledge of substance**—being able to declare the meaning of the text (authorial generalizations) and how the structure helped to shape the content to create and communicate this meaning (structural generalizations).

Inquiry Square

Reproduce this square to help you plan your teaching of a genre that is unfamiliar to your students. Remember that like any reader, students must use all four kinds of knowledge as they read!

Declarative Knowledge	Procedural Knowledge	
4 How can students be helped to articulate the meaning of the text?	3 How can students be helped to put the content they are reading into a mental structure suggested by the author?	FORM
5 How can students be helped to name the structure of the text and how this construction helped communicate the author's meaning?	2 How can students be helped to get the stuff? i.e., access the necessary background information and knowledge that must be brought to bear?	SUBSTANCE
1 **Knowledge of purpose:** What is the purpose and function of reading and writing this kind of text?		

(For more on using the inquiry square to plan instruction, see Wilhelm, Smith & Fredricksen, 2012)

Or, you might instead brainstorm genre elements lists like those that follow on pages 145–148. The lists will get you started in thinking about the expectations of certain text types and in turn, how you might highlight them for students.

Task-Specific or Text-Specific? Teasing Apart Two Terms

I've already blown a lot of hot air earlier in this book about task-specific expectations, but let me review here. A task-specific expectation is when an author uses a particular kind of convention, like irony or symbolism, or when a text is written in such a way that requires a reader to make inferences or find an implied central focus. These conventions, and their associated "task" for the reader trying to interpret and make meaning of them, can move across text types. For example, symbolism is often used in lyric poetry, short stories, and novels and sometimes in informational writing. Inferring is a task required by most literature and is required less in informational texts, where everything important is typically made clear.

When a text type always (or generally) uses a particular kind of convention then the interpretative strategy required by it is considered to be one of the text type or genre expectations. Most text types require the same processes every time you read that genre, and quite often these processes are unique to reading this kind of text, as you will see below when we explore reading fables and arguments, as well as other texts.

A student reads a ballad. When students arrive in the intermediate grades, the texts we ask them to read are often new to them and require them to employ specialized strategies that they probably do not yet know.

The Inquiry Square: A Teacher's Example

Declarative Knowledge	Procedural Knowledge	
Student names the features of the fable including animals as symbols of foibles, ends in moral, etc.	How to put the substance of the proposed fable in an appropriate form: • What animals could represent the foible and other contrasting values? • What actions and key details could show the consequences of this foible? Initial situation, complication by foible, climax, consequences. • Events must be a syllogism leading to a conclusion that can be summarized as a moral. • A moral is one sentence that directly reflects the trajectories of the fable's action.	FORM
Knowledge of the content of particular fables. Knowledge of the moral and how the fable was structured to express this meaning.	How to produce the substance of fables: brainstorming for human qualities that are immoral or irritating. Generate foibles and their concomitant actions, etc. Choose a big one that causes problems for self and others. Choose a foible that is correctable. Think about how people with this foible act and what problems are caused by these actions.	SUBSTANCE
Fables make fun of human shortcomings. Fables show different and better ways of being. Fables can make fun of authorities or specific people, but in a secret way they won't recognize.		KNOWLEDGE OF PURPOSE

- Why write or read this kind of text?
- How can we get the "stuff" to write or read this? (Inquiry?)
- What do we have to do with the "stuff" to make it an argument, satire, table, etc.?

Genre Characteristics Chart

Following is an overview of some genres (text-types) that are often read by students and text-specific processes a reader uses to read them. As you introduce a genre to kids, develop such lists of characteristics with your students. Through think-alouds and other lessons, model how you pay attention to these features to help you read and enjoy the text.

Mystery

The Basic Definition

- A subgenre of narrative fiction; often thought of as a detective story.

- Usually involves a mysterious death or a crime to be solved. In a closed circle of suspects, each suspect must have a credible motive and a reasonable opportunity for committing the crime. The central character must be a detective who eventually solves the mystery by logical deduction from facts fairly presented to the reader. This classic structure is the basis for hundreds of variations on the form.

Purpose

To engage in and enjoy solving a puzzle. Explore moral satisfaction (or dissatisfaction) at resolution. Consider human condition and how to solve or avoid human problems.

Tip-Offs
(also known as Rules of Notice)

- Mystery, crime, or another puzzle to be solved.

- Main character who is a detective who sets out to solve a mystery.

- Suspects and their motives; these must be weighed and evaluated.

- Overt clues about the crime are presented.

- Hidden evidence is presented, i.e., essential details are offered in such a way that they seem unimportant.

- Inference gaps—mysteries, by their very nature, do not tell the whole story. It is up to readers to notice the gaps in the story and try to fill these gaps by using and connecting the information that is presented.

- Suspense—having to hold various possible conclusions at bay as you wait to see what happens; reader is expected to enjoy the suspense, and to read to find out what will happen.

- Foreshadowing—clues left by the author as to possible outcomes.

- Red herring—a kind of foreshadowing clue that leads the reader to false conclusions.

What a Mystery Requires of a Reader

The reader's job is to put the puzzle pieces offered by the author together to figure out the mystery, to appreciate the detective's craft, and to take moral satisfaction from the solution to the mystery. To do this, readers must notice and make meaning with the codes offered above, i.e., they must notice the various forms of evidence and evaluate them; they must notice inference gaps and try to fill them.

Biography

The Basic Definition

- A subgenre of narrative nonfiction/historical nonfiction.

- Presents the facts about an individual's life and makes an attempt to interpret those facts, explaining the person's feelings and motivations. Good biographers use many research tools to gather and synthesize information about their subject, including the person's words, actions, journals, reactions, related books, interviews with friends, relatives, associates and enemies, historical context, psychology, and primary source documents.

Purpose

Often to understand the person and the events and history affected by that person, as well as how historical contexts and events affect individuals.

Tip-Offs

- Often starts with birth or early life and often covers birth-to-death.

- Often delves in to a person's formative years, exploring early influences on a subject's later life.

- Situates person's life in historical terms and a cultural context.

- Uses direct quotes from person and those who knew her.

- Sometimes uses fictionalized scenes/dialogues but always based on what is known about the person and the events described.

- Often uses pictures, maps, photographs, or other historically available documents.

- Biographer possesses a point of view, a larger agenda, and a purpose in reporting on the person's life.

What a Biography Requires of a Reader

Reader should consider author's purpose in presenting the biography. Is it idealized? fair? Why or why not? Is bio a hatchet job? Why? Who is the biographer? When was this biography written? How does this affect my reading of it? How does this help me to understand the influence of this person on history, and history and culture's effect on her? How might this person be a model for things to do or not do in my own life?

Tall Tales

The Basic Definition

A subgenre of narrative fiction/folktales. One of four categories of folktales generally recognized by folklorists. (Others are the variants of European folktales, such as Jack and the Beanstalk, the folktales of African Americans that grew out of African and European roots; and the tales of Native American groups) Tall tales include "exuberant combinations of fact with outrageous fiction." The tales feature an "improvement" on actual happenings. The contrast between fact and fiction is enhanced by giving the story a realistic framework and by a deadpan storytelling style.

Purpose

To entertain, celebrate cleverness of hero, imagine "What If?" and show resilience of the group he represents.

Tip-Offs

- Realism combined with outrageous exaggeration.

- Often reflects the hardships endured by the American settlers.

- Heroes embody courage, brute force, cleverness, as well as the virtues of thrift, hard work, and perseverance.

Fables

The Basic Definition

A short tale used to teach a moral lesson, often with animals as characters.

Purpose

To instruct, to teach humans a lesson about recognizing and overcoming their foibles; to critique authority figures in humorous and anonymous ways; to poke fun.

Tip-Offs

- The story is very brief.

- Main characters are usually animals and are characterized quickly with a few broad strokes.

- One animal/character usually displays the vice or foible being critiqued. This foible is what brings embarrassment or a downfall to the character and this conclusion leads directly to the moral, which follows the fable and is stated in one sentence.

What a Fable Requires of a Reader

The reader must pay attention to the title, which will cue who or what to pay attention to. Then the reader must figure out the symbolic value of each animal or character— what human trait does each represent? The reader must recognize the introductory situation and what causes the complication and consequences. He reads moral and understands how the events of the story, particularly the conclusion, lead to and mirror the instructive statement summarized by the moral. Reader should consider how the moral might apply to his own life.

Arguments

The Basic Definition

The process of presenting or comprehending a reasoned and evidence-based case.

Purpose

To inquire into problems and possible solutions, to persuade or convince others to change belief or take action, to try and get one's way!

Tip-Offs

- A need or desire for something new or for something to change is expressed.

- This assertion is supported through the use of evidence and warrants (reasoning) explaining how the evidence leads to this claim.

- Something is being promoted. (Advertisements almost always contain an argument. Argument is incorporated into many forms of propaganda and persuasion.)

What an Argument Requires of a Reader

The reader must first understand what is being claimed and what is at stake. What will happen or follow if we agree with or reject the argument? If others agree with or reject the argument? Then, the reader must recognize and evaluate the evidence and how it is explained or linked to the claim. The reader may want to express reservations and see if these are or could be responded to. Ultimately, the reader must decide if she is compelled by the argument and if so, what she should believe and do as a result.

Satires

The Basic Definition

A text that uses irony, sarcasm, and ridicule to expose and make fun of human folly and vice.

Purpose

To critique the status quo, to make fun of others and the self, and to offer renewed alternatives and possibilities for being different.

Tip-Offs

- Something is being made fun of, irony is being used, there is a tone of mockery or derision, perhaps the author seems to be supporting a point of view that you cannot expect her to seriously support.

What a Satire Requires of a Reader

The reader must discern what is being made fun of and what possible alternatives are being offered. The reader must decide what is not under dispute in the text, what is under dispute, and how to reconstruct the real implied meaning behind the false satiric meanings being literally presented by the author.

Helping Kids Read Genres
That Are New to Them: The Basics

Whether you use an inquiry square, a genre chart, or something else to plan your teaching, it is essential that you teach the specifics of reading the specific genre that you assign until students have mastered deep understanding of how the genre works. I cannot overemphasize this! Students cannot comprehend or compose texts of a particular type if they do not understand that text and its attendant conventions. To identify the text features and teach them, the first step is to read through several examples of a text type carefully before giving an example of it to students, thinking through all the knowledge and processes you are using to comprehend it. Then, you will probably plan your teaching along these lines:

- Read several examples with the entire class.
- Do a think-aloud or a talkback of some kind with the examples.
- Figure out what is always required of readers of that genre. When you introduce a new text type/genre, simplify it to its most basic structures and features. These are what you will first teach students to attend to. Later, more sophisticated features—and the ways to interpret and critique them—can be introduced.
- Practice using the moves that are required by the genre.
- Try to write an example of the text type using all the conventions required by that genre. Model this for students (you might collaborate on one as a class) before inviting them to do it.

Reading Fables: An Example of Teaching a Genre

Anchor Standards
for Writing, 3

A fable is a good genre to teach because it is accessible and because fables are usually short, so students can gain lots of practice with various examples in a brief amount of time. Through lots of practice with short works, you can build students' skills for use in longer works. For example, the text demands of fables include task-specific processes such as interpreting symbolism and reading for a main idea that can transfer to many other kinds of reading, and to other specific genres like allegories. If kids have trouble or make mistakes, it's not a big deal; you can help correct problems and quickly move on to another example.

Fables address concepts about central human issues and concerns, of course, and thus easily fit into units of study and inquiry of many different kinds. Fables are also fabulous (if you'll excuse the etymological pun!) for teaching how to read for main idea/theme/central focus because they lead pointedly to a moral, which is usually directly expressed. Morals can be deleted and students can write their own and debate relative merits of how well each one matches the plot trajectory and summarizes the implications and central focus of the fable. Fables also show students how stories can be used to make points and cases for particular ways of thinking and being—which we might embrace or disagree with—and therefore encourage authorial reading.

So, the first thing I do with my students is to ask: What is the purpose of writing a fable? We often read a couple and brainstorm why the author might have written it and what work was or could be accomplished by the fable. We then spend a few minutes brainstorming in their notebooks possible purposes of writing a fable.

I then ask: What is it that you have to know and do to write or read a fable? With this question in mind, I might have them read another fable or two.

Here's the conversation my students and I had after they read "The Man With Two Wives," "Venus and the Cat," and "The Lion in Love" and brainstormed about both the purposes of the fables and the features that they all shared.

Tony: Well, fables are good for making fun of mistakes.

Melissa: And more than that… the mistakes they [people] repeat. Their screw-ups, their personality defects.

Tom: I think the point is to understand our faults so we can make them better.

JW: So fables might help us improve ourselves, or tell others how to improve! [Jeff writes all ideas on board.] What else?

Joe: They all end with a bang.

Melissa:	And that ending leads to the point—the part that tells you what you should do.
JW:	The moral.
Melissa:	Yeah....
JW:	[A bit later in conversation] Okay, now we have a good list of some of the possible purposes of writing and reading fables, and we've decided we're going to write some fables to draw attention to problems in the school. Before we get started, what do we have to think about?
Jayne:	Who's gonna read these?
JW:	Right. Who will be the audience?
Jamal:	And why will they read them and what do we want to happen because they read them?
Riley:	Hey, jump back! What are the issues we're going to write about? We never talked about that!
Jamal:	And what we want to change? If it's something that can't be changed, then why write the fable?
Riley:	You da man, Jamal! But how we gonna know if the thing can be changed or not?
JW:	By doing a little bit of research!
Students:	[Groan!]
Jamal:	You mean talk to the principal and stuff?
JW:	No, I mean brainstorming right here what issues bug us about the school, and then brainstorming which ones could be changed if they were just brought to people's attention and possible alternatives were provided.

The students did an excellent job of figuring out purposes of fables and then began to figure out how to decide what to write about and how to get the information they needed (the procedural knowledge of substance).

We then brainstormed how to put what they might learn into the form of a fable. They brainstormed these ideas, which I wrote on the board:

- Figure out animals or other characters that suggest various human values, including the foibles to be addressed (symbolism).
- Animals must exhibit human values but not be humans (not smoke cigars or drink coffee).
- Figure out a sequence of events involving the characters that will make a particular point about the consequences of certain attitudes or behaviors.
- Title that describes the main character and his or her problem or that describes the problem or issue being examined.
- Begin fable by introducing situation.
- Immediately proceed to complication, the problem or issue at play.
- Major character makes decision or takes action.
- Decision or action leads to a clear set of consequences.
- The action of the story and its consequences imply a clear moral.
- This syllogism of events leading to a conclusion must be summarized in a moral.
- What makes a good moral? We must consider phrasing and content.

To conclude the day's lesson, I asked students to think about what we would expect our readers to think and do as they read our fables and how we were going to help them think and do these things.

Talkbacks

Sometimes I have students do a think-aloud of the text type I'm introducing. Because fables are short, students might read several and compare to find what moves and strategies are always required. Or different students could read different fables and strategies could be compared.

Another option is to have students read one and then do a talkback of their reading. Here's a general guide for such a talkback, along with some of Jamal's specific comments during a talkback about Aesop's "The Man with Two Wives." I always organize talkbacks along the five dimensions of activity highlighted by the inquiry square (see page 142). Jamal's responses to the prompts he was given are in italics:

Talkback for Fable Reading

(The talkback enacts procedural knowledge of substance, since it prompts students to access meaning and articulate that meaning and how it was created.)

1 The talkback reflects knowledge of the genre's purpose.
For example, what work can this genre get done for writers and readers?

Like we said, fables are about foibles! The purpose is to make fun of some human weakness—but not too harshly so people will still be open and to show a better way to be. So fables are about making fun and changing things, especially how people behave!

2 The talkback reflects knowledge of the substance of the text and the topic or general subject explored by this substance.
For example, what was the topic of the fable—the problem or issue it examines?

This fable is about a dude who had two wives. He took too much on his plate. It's kind of like about what Jesus said about serving two masters!!! You just can't do it!

3 The talkback connects the student's prior knowledge to the text.
For example, what background knowledge about the topic helped me to read this? What did I have to know and bring to the text so it would make sense and connect to my life and activity?

When I read this I thought about when I tried to run track and play baseball at the same time last spring... Different kinds of friends and they want to do different things. (Jamal uses procedural knowledge of substance by accessing his relevant experiences.)

4 The talkback shows the student how to access and comprehend the coded meanings of the text. It reveals that the student has the tools to understand the text and to play the part of the audience for whom the text was written.

5 The talkback recognizes and names global (and perhaps local) embedded structures and conventions of the text. For example, I knew it was a fable because... Fables start this way and then... Fables make use of animals to symbolize...

I knew this was a fable because we've been studying them. Plus it started with a title, was really short, it didn't have any animals which is kind of funny, but it had this guy who made a big mistake and his two wives kept takin' bites out of him and it had a little old moral at the end and that clinches it. It's a fable. It's a little story that holds up the mirror because it's about typical situations. We're supposed to learn from his mistakes being held up to the old microscope. (Jamal taps into declarative knowledge of form by recognizing and articulating the genre tip-offs and expectations. At the same time he uses procedural knowledge of form—what you do to respond to and make meaning of particular structures and codes.)

6 **The talkback includes references to the process of reading.**
For example, when I read this, I was sure to do certain things as a reader like ___. Because it was a fable and I know the animals are symbolic of human foibles, I figured out that the fox symbolized being sly or cunning ___. A part that was hard for me to understand was... so I ___. I reread the part about... because ___.

I was lookin' for the lesson from the very start. I knew somebody was gonna make a big mistake and get squeezed and go down and that Aesop was gonna pass big-time judgment on him! (Jamal uses procedural knowledge of form because he recognizes the form and initiates processes for fulfilling the formal expectations, i.e., appreciating how the events lead to the moral.)

7 **The talkback includes an adequate retelling of surface and deep meaning.** It summarizes the key points to remember, including:

- introduction to situation
- key details; main events and consequences of them
- moral and how it follows from the story action

Remember that it is in your own words, though vocabulary from the story may be used.

This guy married two babes, one old and one young. I don't know how he swung that, but he did. But the problems started because the young one pulled out his grey hairs cause she didn't want him lookin' like some old dude. But the old one pulled out his black hairs because she didn't want him lookin' young and sexy like me, I'm guessing! So the guy ends up bald. So the moral follows on all of that... you try to do too much, you get pulled too many ways, then you lose whatever you had. (Jamal uses declarative knowledge of substance by articulating the surface and deep meaning of the fable, which he was able to deduce by using the required reading processes—by understanding the substance and how it was structured to make a particular point.)

(For a book-length treatment about teaching specific kinds of narratives, see Fredrickson, Wilhelm and Smith, 2012)

Reading News Stories

Anchor Standards
for Writing, 2

News writing is a kind of simple informational writing that students need to know how to read for real-life purposes. I think that it is very important that students from upper elementary on become familiar with the newspaper and its various kinds of stories. The most basic story, of course, is the news story. I use news stories throughout my teaching to connect our studies to current events, to add new information and breadth to our classroom inquiries, and to teach reading strategies. I also often have students write news stories about their reading, since it gives such great practice in identifying key details, writing summaries, considering deep meaning, etc.

The conventions of news writing range from the simple to the more complex. On the declarative level, student writers need to know that news is a report about a recent and noteworthy event; that it must include the five W's and H (who, what, where, why, when, and how) to comprehensively cover the event; that the purpose is to interest and inform the reader; and that there are structural elements such as the headline, the lead, the body, and possible other elements such as quotations, call-outs, and so on.

On the procedural level, writers need to know how to inquire into the events and issues they will report on… through investigation, interviewing, databases, fact files, and more. They need to know what constitutes unbiased, comprehensive reporting and what does not. They need to learn how to put the substance they have learned into a form including a headline, lead, and a body that covers the five W's and H, and so forth.

Later on, they'll learn about different kinds of news stories, like the death story, the meeting story, the sports story, the advance or follow-up story, and variations and extensions on the news like features, editorials, and reviews, all of which have particular purposes and codes.

Once they understand how such stories are produced, they will know what to attend to and critique as readers. At first, though, I attend to the general news story.

Questions to Guide Reading General News Stories

1 What's the topic of the article?
The main topic of this article is ___. Tip-offs: The headline and first paragraph confirm this topic by ___.

2 What important ideas are expressed about the topic?
The five W's and H are ___. The most important ideas to remember are ___.

3 **Does it clearly make known how this event/issue relates to other events and issues, in the past and future?** In other words, does it have important "global" implications? How should it help me think about things that are important?

This article was important to read because ___. It connects to and will influence future issues like ___ by ___.

4 **Is the story coherent? Do all the story ideas relate to each other?** *The ideas covered were all about making the point that ___. This helps the reader to understand that ___ were organized around the topic/central issue of ___.*

5 **What reading strategies am I using to create meaning? What tools am I using as I critique the structure, the writing, or the content of the piece?** *When I read this article I had to do certain things/make certain moves as a reader, such as ___.*

News stories are a type of general expository text that lays out information. Because news stories are short, students can get repeated practice with techniques that can help them in reading more extended informational texts, such as textbooks. The following guide can be used to help students with any kind of expository text.

Questions to Guide Reading General Exposition/Information Texts

1 **What's the topic?**
This text was about the topic of ___.

2 **What's the author's purpose?**
The author probably wrote this for the purpose of ___.

3 **How does the structure of the piece serve its purpose? How does the organization of the piece serve the purpose?**
The author chose the form of ___ to meet her purpose because ___.

4 **What are its main points?**
The main points the author wants us to remember and carry away with us are ___.

5 What new ideas does it convey? What parts interested me?

Ideas that I learned that surprised and interested me were ___.

6 What did I do as I read to help me understand? What did I do as I critiqued it?

Things I did that helped me read this text and figure out what I thought about it were ___.

7 After reading the text, what questions do I want to ask the author?

I'd like to ask the author some additional questions, and I'd like to know more about ___ and know what she thinks about ___ and ask why she wrote it in this particular way.

8 What does this piece do for me? How does it change my thinking about this topic or other topics? What does it make me want to do? To learn more about? How does it influence my own life and future?

I'm going to use this text to think about/write about/do these things ___.

Obviously, not all prompts need to be used or responded to. Prompts can be rephrased and adapted depending on the text, and engagement and capacity of your students.

(For a book-length treatment of instructional ideas to teach specific kinds of informational and expository text structures, see Fredrickson, Wilhelm and Smith, 2012.)

Looking at the Elements of Argument

Anchor Standards for Writing, I

Perhaps the most important kind of text to be able to read or write, both for disciplinary learning and democratic life, is the argument. Newspapers, textbooks, magazines, and Web sites are full of arguments. Advertisements are perhaps the most ubiquitous form of argument. Think-alouds can be used to figure out what must be done to recognize, read, and critique an argument.

Now, arguments can seem daunting to teach and read, but I have found that the fourth and fifth graders with whom I work are quickly able to understand and use arguments with great facility. So hang on and bear with me here!

According to the logician Stephen Toulmin and other philosophers of argument, on the basic level, arguments consist of a claim, data, and warrants. (I'm grateful to George Hillocks, 1995; Michael Smith, 1998; and to Maine Writing Project Fellow Lori Power, who adapted George's and Michael's ideas in the following way to create

Here we collaboratively create an argument using notecards that feature different elements of an argument.

a teaching demonstration on reading advertisements as argument. The five questions in bold on page 161 are from Michael Smith's presentation.)

To simplify the terms a bit, an argument starts with a claim and a position that will be argued for. This is also known as a thesis. With younger students, instead of using the term "claim" I might just ask: What are you arguing for? What do you want the reader to be convinced of: to know, believe or do? Data is simply evidence. Any facts that can be used to support (or not support) the claim can be considered data. The younger students I work with all understand the word evidence, though I tend to use the term data with older students. Warrants are explanations of how the evidence supports the claim. With younger students I simply ask them to "explain the evidence."

Arguments begin and are grounded in evidence. The situation (data) provides the reason to make an argument in the first place. That is, there is a problem and we need to do something. The evidence (data) supports the claim about what needs to be done.

Arguments are generally made because conditions cause us to desire something we lack or threaten something we value. Since data specify these conditions, they are the concrete facts and details indicating that things aren't as they should be or that they could be different. Students are often surprised to learn that the same data can support entirely different claims, depending on the warrants—the explanations and reasoning invoked and cultural values linked to the data.

Model the Process

Modeling how you attend to these features of argument in your own think-alouds helps students understand what to notice and how to judge and interpret these conventions. Cueing students to attend to claims, data, and warrants in their own think-alouds, and helping them to ask the right questions about these features, helps them to become critical consumers of arguments.

For Students Well-Versed in the Elements of Argument

A bit more advanced argument may include backing, reservations, or qualifiers; and a response to reservations or rebuttal. But again, I would not pursue these more sophisticated conventions with students until they have mastered the basic ones. If some students are ready for these more advanced features, then I would certainly introduce these to them as I continued to work with other students on the basic features.

Backing is used when a warrant needs support. Readers ask an author: "How do you know the backing supports the truth of the warrant?"

Backing is used if the warrant is not familiar or compelling to the audience. For instance, animal rights activists must confront a very powerful argument by medical researchers that testing on animals is warranted by the value of human life. They may need to back their own warrants by convincing the audience that when we cherish the lives of all creatures, great and small, we deepen and enrich our own lives and increase the value of human life. Medical researchers, on the other hand, might back their warrant by citing evidence of human suffering that was alleviated, diseases cured, lives extended as a result of their research, and evidence that human suffering continues in many cases because of animal rights. There is a current television ad campaign in which drug companies use such backing.

Reservations are arguments against the claim. The arguer may want to address these up front with a response. Readers must ask: "Are all reservations addressed?" and: "Does the response adequately address the reservation?"

Qualifiers are limits placed on the argument; for instance, if there are limits to the claim or if it applies only in certain instances. For example, researchers might qualify their argument to ensure the humane care of animals as long as it does not impede research. Animal rights advocates may grant the qualification that when humanity is in dire need, researchers might temporarily suspend certain restrictions.

Introducing Argument: Sixth Graders Talk Back to Madison Avenue

The sixth grade is involved in an inquiry unit about how to best protect the environment, and we're studying argument because we are all going to write arguments about an ecological topic of interest to us. To study argument, we've been looking at advertisements to tease out the argument that each one makes. Here's Carrie having a go at an ad she found in *People* persuading readers to subscribe to *Money* magazine. She's using a talkback guide to help her identify the tip-off that the ad's structure is an argument and to help her identify and evaluate elements of an argument like claims, data, and warrants. The guide helps readers to recognize and interpret important genre conventions, thereby guiding their reading and critique of a particular text.

> *All it says is, 'Why live paycheck to paycheck when you can live dividend to dividend?' And then it says, 'Money. You need this magazine.' Okay, that's the tip-off. They want us to buy the magazine. I think the claim is that we . . . lack money. Ha! They're right about that! No . . . the claim is . . . errr. That we need Money . . . the magazine, I mean. Because if you read Money then, ummm, you will earn so much from investing that you'll be all set. Yeah. Okay, as for data . . . what makes me think this claim is right? What supports it? Well, there . . . geezum . . . there isn't any data. There isn't anything! There's no warrants either . . . there's nothing that explains the data . . . But then there isn't any data, just a claim!!! This ad is just a claim. There's nothing that supports it. There is no reason in the world I should believe this ad. I wonder why they think this kind of ad would even work?*

Carrie exhibits a knowledge of how arguments work and can see that this ad makes an implicit argument through a simple suggestion that it does not back up. Here's an example of an argument from a student editorial (Michael Smith, 1998):

Claim: (Reader recognizes claim and the text as an argument in service of that claim.) The school should have a smoking area.

Data: (Reader asks: "What makes you say so?") Neighbors are complaining about kids smoking near the school grounds. In other schools, smoking areas have decreased complaints about smoking near school.

Warrant: (Reader asks: "So What?" What values or principles support the evidence's connection to the claim) The school should try to reduce neighbor's complaints.

Backing: (Reader asks: "How do you know? What makes you say so?") So neighbors will support school activities.

Audience: I don't care if neighbors support school activities.

Backing: If they don't, they won't vote for the school levy.

Audience: I don't share your value about neighbors voting for the school levy.

Backing: If they don't vote for the levy, teachers will not get raises and sports and arts programs will be cancelled. (backing must continue until the audience shares your valuing of the data.)

Reservation: (Reader asks if all counter-arguments are fairly cited.) We could increase security around the school and that would solve the problem without a smoking area.

Response/Rebuttal: (Reader asks if response addresses reservation.) The school has no jurisdiction off of school property, so we can't increase security there.

Talkback Guide for Argument

A talkback guide is a great way to get kids to notice and interpret the different features of an argument.

1 Reader asks: Does the argument report the data?
The data and evidence presented are...

  a. *Reader asks: Is the data persuasive? Is more information needed to establish the data? (An argument can't be advanced unless the audience accepts the data as reliable and compelling.)*

The information is persuasive/unpersuasive or sufficient/insufficient because...

2 Reader asks: Is the evidence supported and explained by warrants?
The evidence is linked to the claim by these warrants and explanations...

  a. *Reader asks if the warrants are clear. Does the warrant connect the evidence to the claim with values and reasoning? Does the warranting justify the leap to the conclusion?*

The warrants are clear and convincing/unclear and unconvincing because...

3 **Cites the backing for warrants, if necessary.**
The backing for the warrants is/are...

  a. *Reader asks if the backing supports, with specifics, the truth or acceptability of the warrant.*

The backing helps me to value the evidence by... or does not help me to value the evidence because...

4 **Qualifier or reservations are listed.**
The reservations to the argument are...

  a. *Has the arguer considered all of the objections which the audience can make against the claim? Have the reservations been adequately responded to?*

The reservations are adequately/inadequately addressed by...

5 **Claim is cited.**
What is it you should believe or do? What is it you lack? What threatens you? What is it you need? What is the reader being asked to know, believe, or do? The claim is clearly stated as... /is implied to be...

  a. *Whether the argument is convincing and why is explained. What worked and did not work for you as a reader? Where was the author convincing and not convincing? What will you do or think in the future as a result of this argument?*

I was convinced/unconvinced by the argument because... and this argument will inform my thinking and action in the future by...

(For a book-length treatment of instruction on teaching specific kinds of argument, see Smith, Wilhelm, and Fredricksen, 2012)

The Ultimate Conclusion of Reading

I always conclude informational readings by asking students if they can assimilate (take the new information they have just read) and apply it to already well-established schema (personal knowledge structures organized around the topic) that they already possess—in the case that the new information adds to but supports or abets what they already knew—or if they had to accommodate the new information (use the new information to make a completely new structure, or to overhaul an old one by restructuring it—in the case when you did not know much about the topic or have been convinced that your previous knowledge was faulty or inadequate). Another

Nate offers a compelling piece of evidence as part of a debate about a fable's best moral.

option is that students found the new information was not new, was not compelling, or was faulty, in which case it will be discarded.

As is always the case after teaching new strategies, structure reflection into your lessons—ask when students might apply this information or strategy in another text or life situation. Getting them to make those predictions and connections helps activate the strategies for possible transfer. Jamal achieved such transfer. He recognized the higher purposes of fables and also how different kinds of writing could be used in repressive situations to work for change. To show these understandings when reflecting on our fable reading and writing, he wrote this poem:

> I thought fables were just for school
> But I was wrong, fables can be cool
> They can help you get justice and speak what's true
> And let people know what they never knew
> Though it might sound strange
> Fables can do your work for change
> And this is hip:
> you can stay out of trouble too—
> If nobody knows the author was you!

CHAPTER 9

MAKING IT MEANINGFUL
Using Think-Alouds for Performance-Based Assessment

I n this chapter we'll explore how formative performance-based assessments can inform and move towards meaningful performance-based summative assessments, assessments that are sorely needed to complement standardized tests, and other procedures that can only measure recall.

CCSS

Helping teachers meet Anchor Standards for Reading, 7–9 and students meet Anchor Standards for Reading, 4–10

After my student Walter made his reading activity known to me with a think-aloud, I began to point out all the expert strategies he was using as a reader. At one point, this struggling seventh grader interrupted me and with a surprised expression dancing across his face said,

"Hey, maybe I *can* get good at this!"

"Of course you can!" I replied. "You already are good at a lot of things about reading and you already can do a lot of things that expert readers do."

"But how come I always feel so dumb after tests and things?" he asked.

"Because the tests are dumb. Good tests should show you what you can do as well as what you need to work on. Good tests should make you feel smart!"

Our conversation continued, and I wrapped it up by naming a few strategies I felt Walter was ready to use. We set the goal for him to try one or two of these strategies during the next passage he read. Walter, usually resistant to reading, was eager to read that day and happy. We had celebrated him as a reader, and we had provided a new challenge that would help his competence grow in a visible, useful, and immediately apparent way.

This concluding chapter will show how think-alouds can be used as motivating, effective assessment tools. As I hope my exchange with Walter showed, they can be used to make strengths apparent to students and a cause for celebration. Think-alouds can also map out avenues of progress for students, displaying what they could try next—and showing how to do so in a meaningful context.

Think-Alouds: Assessing Knowledge in Performance

Q&A 5: How can think-alouds be used as an assessment tool?

Think-alouds provide a performance-based assessment. They offer an in-process look at readers engaged in comprehension activity. In comparison, quizzes and tests only look at an end product of comprehension, usually only literal comprehension, and don't provide an assessment of the powerful, process-oriented meaning-making tools of readers.

Tests, particularly standardized ones, also cannot hope to show the growth that occurs when students take the risk to try new strategies that they haven't quite mastered and that don't yet lead to the richest possible interpretation. Growth occurs through these kinds of risky leaps, but mastering the new strategies takes time.

As a parent, when I receive report cards on my children, it strikes me anew that grades tell us little beyond the most general impression a teacher has of a child's performance. I most value a narrative assessment that describes in specific detail what my child has been working on, her strengths and weaknesses, ways that I can help out, and what will be worked on next in school. Think-alouds can provide the specific information necessary for writing such assessments, and think-alouds can be appended to assessments so that I can get a real flavor of what my child is doing as she reads.

As a teacher, I feel the same way. Grades, tests, and quizzes often don't teach my students much and often do not describe them very well or help me to teach them better. I much prefer performance-based assessments that will help me to do my job in a more wide-awake, wide-aware, knowledgeable, and powerful way.

Here is another thing: the next generation of assessments, including the Smarter Balanced and DARCC tests for the Common Core, require both problem-solving and reflections/process analyses, justifying how the performance task was completed. Think alouds are point-on preparation for these new assessments.

Seeing improvement energizes teachers and learners. Think-alouds can show proof of student strategy use and progress. This kind of evidence can be used to augment other forms of assessment and replace them to some degree. Having kids keep lists of the strategies they have used, both in general and with particular texts, is a way to keep track of their growth and to remind them what they can do and should do as readers.

The following guidelines will be helpful whenever you engage in a think-aloud with a student. Refer to them as you study a think-aloud transcript, or when you talk it over with a student, or even use these guidelines to ask students to assess themselves. They will provide rich feedback and fodder for both assessment and planning. Obviously you would not use all of these at the same time; you would pick and choose the guidelines that you are helping a student to work on. What I've tried to do here is to cite a full range of strategic knowledge and expertise that think-alouds can help you to assess.

A Boon to Teacher Research

Because think-alouds are so effective for assessing students' reading and learning in specific ways, they are also great tools for teacher research, or more informally, assessing one's instruction. In my own teaching, I use think-alouds

- to quickly assess students' reading on particular tasks.

- to use this feedback to inform my instructional planning: whole-class, small-group, and individual instruction.

- to see how to group kids with similar needs for specific small-group instruction; to see when to change these groups.

- to give students a way to self-assess their current situation and growth as readers.

- to help students assess each other and share appropriate strategies.

- to build student portfolios and my teaching portfolio.

- to assess student improvement over time; to get a timeline of reading improvement.

- to provide data for written assessments and comments.

- to do case studies on readers with difficulties in order to help them.

- as a teacher research tool during small classroom studies about particular kinds of reading or teaching interventions. (Please see *You Gotta BE the Book* for a description of how teacher research can work in this way.)

What to Watch For: Questions to Help Assess Reading

Following are some of the reading strategies and behaviors that you can assess with think-alouds:

1 Does the reader understand her purposes for reading a particular text?

____ Is the purpose personal?

____ Is the purpose socially significant?

____ Does the purpose consider a task that the reading can help to complete?

____ How can the reading be made more purposeful?

2 Does the reader understand (or attempt to understand) the purposes and goals of the author?

CCSS

Anchor Standard
for Reading, 6

3 Does the reader bring personal background knowledge to bear in understanding the text?

____ What are the reader's primary sources of information about the world? about the text?

____ How are these sources brought to bear during the reading act?

____ How might the use of these information sources be expanded or assisted?

4 How well does the reader bring knowledge forward from one part of the text to another, from one text or activity to another text or activity?

CCSS

Anchor Standards
for Reading, 4–9

____ Can the reader retell, talk back, or paraphrase?

____ Can the reader make connections between different pieces of information from separate parts of the text to make inferences, or see coherent patterns?

5 How well does the reader employ other general processes of reading?

____ Does the student have high expectations of print?

____ Does the student predict and verify predictions?

____ Does the reader ask questions and interrogate text?

____ What kinds of questions are asked?

___ Are question types varied to kind of text?

___ Does the reader ask inference questions? author and me questions? on-my-own or world questions?

___ Does the reader ask for help? ask stimulating questions of self and others?

___ Does the reader ask questions and make connections that help apply what is read to the real world? that transfer new processes of reading to new texts?

___ Does the reader respond emotionally?

___ Does the reader visualize settings, situations, characters of story? form mental representations of informational texts?

___ Does the student have other sensory experiences, hearing dialogue, etc.?

___ Does the reader provide evidence of comprehension monitoring? strategy adjustment?

___ Does the reader identify confusion, ask if it "makes sense," and apply fix-up strategies when needed?

___ Is reading speed varied for different situations? Does the student pause or stop and apply fix-up strategies?

___ How does the student deal with problems and frustration?

___ Are there other strategies that would be helpful to the reader?

CCSS

Anchor Standard for Reading, 10

6 How independent is the reader with a particular text or kind of text?

___ Where is the reader's ZPD?

___ Is the text easy (at the independent level)?

___ Is the text too challenging (at the frustrational level) because the reader does not have necessary background, understanding of purpose, knowledge of vocabulary, knowledge of text type, and attendant codes and strategies expected?

___ If the text is too challenging, can frontloading of content or strategy use make the text accessible in the ZPD?

___ Where are comprehension and engagement faltering?

___ At what point in a particular text is instruction and guidance necessary?

7 **How well does the student understand global structures of organizing text?**

CCSS
Anchor Standards
for Reading, 2, 3, 5

___ Does the reader recognize how particular text types serve different authorial purposes?

___ Does the reader recognize particular text types and how they proceed from beginning to middle to end?

___ Does the reader understand and represent the different ways of presenting textual ideas (chronologically, classification, comparison-contrast, description, argument, etc.) and the uses and strengths of each?

___ Does the student understand the textual expectations (different codes and conventions, and the strategies for recognizing and interpreting these) of particular text types?

___ Is knowledge of text structure used to improve comprehension?

___ Does the student integrate information from various parts of a text?

8 **Does the student recognize text as a construction of an author?**

___ How well does the reader talk back or converse with an author? How often does the reader question, agree, or disagree with an author? Does the student ever talk back to an author?

9 **How well does the reader use local-level coherence to make links within sentences or to connect sentences? to link different parts of a text together?**

CCSS
Anchor Standards
for Reading, 1–3

10 **How well are inference gaps recognized and inferences made?**

11 **How often does the reader encounter unfamiliar words?**

___ What strategies are used to deal with vocabulary challenges?

___ What other strategies could be used?

12 **How well does the student recognize and use particular codes and conventions?**

___ What cues are noticed, used, and not used?

___ How much and what kind of guidance is needed to help the student use them?

13 How wide a variety of strategies are used with particular texts?

___ Poorer readers tend to use only one or two strategies and to use these repeatedly, even when inappropriate. If only a few strategies are used repeatedly, students can use assistance to widen repertoire and to recognize when and how new appropriate strategies may be used. Older poor readers tend to use the same strategies as better readers, but less effectively, appropriately, or flexibly. How can teaching help expand and improve on this?

14 How well does the student learn information from text? learn ways of reading?

___ How well is this transferred and applied to new situations?

___ How can the teacher help assist transfer?

15 How willing is the student to take risks, go beyond the literal text, and hypothesize?

___ Too many text-bound comments work against active comprehension and suggest that the teacher should use interventions to foster hypothesizing, predicting, inferring, elaborating, evaluating, and conversing with author.

16 How does the think-aloud reveal unsuspected strengths?

___ How can these be celebrated and built upon?

Teacher and Student Checksheets

Checksheets are highly adaptable—you can use them to evaluate individual readers, see patterns among students, or you can give them to students for use in evaluating themselves and each other. They can also provide great communication with parents about what you are trying to teach, how well their child is doing, and what they might do at home to help out.

You can use examples like the following, design your own around specific strategies you are trying to teach, or work with your students to design ones for classroom use.

As we saw in the previous chapters, you can create check sheets or talkback prompting guides for use with specific types of tasks like inferring, reading for a main idea, or interpreting symbolism. You can also use them for general processes

General Processes Checksheet

Self-Evaluation	not much	sometimes	often
1. Used personal background knowledge			
2. Made predictions			
3. Corrected predictions			
4. Asked questions			
5. Used images to see			
6. Was aware of problems			
7. Used fix-ups			

of reading, as we saw in Chapter 2, or to prompt and guide students to attend to the features of particular text types, as we saw in Chapter 6. Above is a variation on a general processes checksheet.

As I worked with my young friend Walter throughout one school year, we often used such checksheets. At the beginning of the year, he made only very limited use of the general processes of reading. By helping him to access and develop background knowledge through frontloading, and by prompting him to make and correct predictions through think-alouds and talkback guides, Walter gradually grew as a reader. We bridged from correcting predictions to monitoring comprehension and fix-up strategies. But even after a full semester of intensive work, we could see that he did not ask many questions, nor did he seem to visualize what he read.

The checksheet both summarized what Walter did do as a reader so we could celebrate and consolidate these skills, and also made it obvious to us both that Walter needed more help to visualize what he read. I therefore prompted and guided him through this process with visual protocols and other visualization techniques such as picture mapping and reading manipulatives/symbolic story representations. These techniques allowed us to "see" what Walter was able to visualize as he read and allowed us to assess and chart his progress and celebrate his considerable improvement.

Think-Aloud–Fueled Student Self-Assessments

Not only do we want readers to internalize strategies, but we also want them to internalize critical standards for good and engaged reading. We want them to know when they have read well and when not, as well as what to try in order to read better. It's been a core assumption of this book that if we want kids to get good at something, then we must give them the opportunity to practice it, and we must assist them in doing it. Further, we must name and celebrate real achievements, and set realistic goals and help students to meet them. That's why self-assessment is so important: It gives kids practice in applying these critical standards, which is essential if we want them to become independent readers.

As Grist for Written Reflections

When Branwen, who struggled as a reader, wrote a self-reflection about her think-aloud of "The Chaser," she expressed: "I still pay to much attenshun to my own ideas and not enough to the story. Like when I read about the stairs I thot about how our stairs creak. But I did think about why the stairs creaked in the story, like to tell us this was scary and run-down. So I'm getting better!!! I didn't feel too much, except sorry for the girl who I never really met but no one seems to care about her. I am working on caring about people in stories, which is something I never tried before. The very sweet and bootiful end."

Think-alouds made Branwen's strengths and weaknesses as a reader visible to her. The think-aloud process also supported her as she worked to improve her reading repertoire, and to assess her improvement, which she does here quite movingly.

At the end of the year, Walter told me: "I never knew there was so much to reading. It's kind of like it's both more complicated and easier than I thought before. I mean, it's more complicated because I didn't know all the things you have to do. But it's easier because now I know what to do and so it makes more sense to me."

My Think-Aloud Moves: A Checklist for Students

On the following page is a self-assessment checklist to give to students. Before handing it out to students, list any moves that you want them to make and monitor on the left side. In the middle, students are to check off each time they make the move. On the right, they can make comments regarding how often they make the move, when and why they made the move, questions they have, goals they want to set, and so forth.

Name _____ Date _____

My Think-Aloud Moves

Example:

Move	✓	Comments
1 **Connecting life to reading**		
2 **Making predictions**		
3 **Making inferences**		
a. Filling gaps		
b. Adding things together		
c. Elaborating beyond the story		
4 **Visualizing**		
5 **Summarizing**		
a. Noting key details		
b. Bringing meaning forward		
c. Thinking about the author's message		

I did one for Walter, which read like this:

Name _____ Date _____

My Think-Aloud Moves

Example:

Move	✓	Comments
1 Connecting life to reading	✓	Use pictures from my life to see.
2 Making predictions	✓	I try to figger out what's going to happen.
3 Making inferences		figgering out how to do this.
a. Filling gaps		
b. Adding things together		
c. Elaborating beyond the story		
4 Visualizing	✓✓✓	working on this. getting good at it. Now I read and see like a comic book or seeing a movie.
5 Summarizing		
a. Noting key details	✓	I remember these things when I can picture them.
b. Bringing meaning forward	✓	getting better!
c. Thinking about the author's message		hard!

Improving Comprehension With Think-Aloud Strategies ✦ 2010 Jeffrey Wilhelm, Scholastic ✦ page 173

Coding Think-Alouds

Expert Reader Coding

When students code their own or other students' think-aloud responses, they get into the "secret code" aspect of the endeavor—and vigorously self-assess in the process. My own pre-service teaching students have developed several different coding schemes, and I've read about several others that teachers and researchers use to great effect. So there are lots of possible variations, and you can certainly adapt or create one to fit your own purposes. First the students do their own written or visual think-aloud, then they go back and label, or code, the kinds of moves they have made. See following page for an example of codings for general processes of reading.

Cued Think-Aloud: Coding Conflict Types

A few codes at a time can really go a long way, so try to use codes only for what you are focusing on with students. Invite your students to invent symbols too. Different codes can obviously be developed for general processes or for task-specific processes. Teachers can also code student think-alouds for assessment purposes. I sometimes find it useful during conferences to sit down with a student and code a think-aloud or two together.

PK	applied prior knowledge		**AM**	author-and-me question
=	connected text segment to personal lived experience		**OYO**	on-your-own question
V or 👁	visualized or saw something		**P**	predict
!	emotion of some kind		**PC**	prediction corrected
?	confusion		**T**	topic identified
(?)	asked a question		☆	key detail
RT	right-there/literal question		(☆)	direct statement of main idea or central focus
TS	think-and-search/inference question		**M**	comprehension-monitoring move

Showing how a student's codes for readings of similar texts change over time provides a time-line of reading improvement and progress. This can be powerful and positive for students, teachers, and parents to see.

Lifted Passages

Ask students to "lift" a short passage that gave them particular trouble or that they found particularly challenging, important, and rich from a longer reading such as a chapter. I often assign "passage lifter" as a literature circle role when we do this kind of student discussion group. Students can make copies or a transparency of the lifted passage, and the kids can examine the passage together to discuss monitoring and fix-up strategies that could be used, how what came before and after the passage would aid comprehension, how the role of prior personal and textual knowledge could be played out, and so on. I quite like this technique because admitting confusion and identifying the source of it are two important expert reading strategies that poorer readers lack.

By making the identification of trouble spots an assignment for all readers, admitting confusion becomes part of the accepted classroom project. By sharing how to attack the highlighted problems, students pool expertise, see problems they may not have encountered yet but will at some point, and are involved in an important communal activity of helping each other. If students honestly can't find any passages that gave them trouble, then this is a tip-off that they should be reading a slightly more challenging text.

CHAPTER 10

THINK-ALOUDS AS FORMATIVE ASSESSMENT AND TEACHER RESEARCH

Learning From Our Students How to Best Teach Them

A student in one of my classes said after a think-aloud, "I actually get it...I get it and I get HOW to get it... and I NEVER get it! This is AMAZING!" *Thinking aloud and what happens for students is kind of amazing, isn't it?*

—email from Andrew Porter during our Advanced Reading Institute

Formative assessment can be defined as assessment FOR learning before and during the process of learning instead of the typical summative assessment of learning *after* the process (Lorna Earl, 2003). Formative assessment is for the purpose of naming and celebrating what students know and can do, as well as setting the next appropriate challenge and knowing how to provide the right assistance to meet it. As such, formative assessments work *in service* of learning, they work *for* learning, and they work *to inform* immediate instruction that can continue to support the learning. They are used to gauge progress towards goals and standards. They are not used to pass judgments and assign grades.

Formative assessment also serves the needs of reflective teachers and teacher researchers because they provide us with data, in the process of real learning, that we can use to learn from our students how to teach them better in the next segment of the lesson or unit. It is data at the point of need and the point of use!

Formative assessment gives both students and teacher ongoing feedback for monitoring learning progress during a learning sequence. Think-alouds, because they are a powerful tool for making student thinking, reading, and problem-solving processes visible and available, are a consummate tool of formative assessment.

Assessment for learning... Assessing for learning is analyzing data to help inform the next level of teaching.

Assessment as learning... Emphasizes the role of the student. Students personally monitor what they are learning and use the feedback from this monitoring to make adjustments, adaptations, and even major changes in what they understand. Think-alouds are excellent for fulfilling this purpose. (Earl, 2003)

Anchor Standards for Writing, 7–9 (for teachers), and 1–10 (for students)

Assessment *FOR* and *AS* Learning: FORMATIVE	Assessment *OF* Learning: SUMMATIVE
Strives to increase student achievement	Strives to document student achievement
Diagnoses a student's individual strengths and weaknesses by providing results that are unique to students	Diagnoses a program's strength and weakness by providing comparable results.
Provides data throughout a unit or course of study that allows tailoring of instruction and motivation for improvement. Demonstrates improvement throughout the learning process.	Provides summative results at the end of a unit or course of study
Informs students about themselves and helps them learn how to take charge of their own progress	Informs others (teachers, parents, administrators, community members) about students and their achievement
Assumes the teacher's role is to promote student success.	Assumes the teacher's role is to gauge student success
Reflects knowledge, skills and understanding that underpin standards	Reflects the standards themselves.

> *When the cook tastes the soup, that's formative; when the guests taste the soup, the summative.*
>
> **—Robert Stake**

> *Summative assessment is like an autopsy, formative is the wellness check up.*
>
> **—Cris Tovani**

My argument here is that formative assessment can and should be a form of daily teacher research. It constitutes reflective practice and is necessary to informed practice—learning from your students each day what they have learned and how they learned it and therefore how to best teach them next! Think-alouds have to be in your formative assessment repertoire.

We already have enough summative assessment including many required measures. We need to move from summative assessment *of* learning to more and more formative assessment *as* and *for* learning. Think-alouds help us make this move.

Assessing *for/as/of* Learning

From	To
of	*for/as*
Summative	Formative
Judgments	Descriptions
Comparative	Individual
At the end	Ongoing
Impersonal	Interactive

I have long been arguing that inquiry is the most powerful instructional model (see Wilhelm, 2007 and Wilhelm, Wilhelm and Boas, 2008) and that think-alouds are a way of promoting reading as inquiry. We need to foreground our purpose in teaching any unit or lesson (i.e., what are our major conceptual and procedural goals—to be actualized in the culminating project) and then to ask how our assessment throughout and after the unit reflects and serves these goals. Thinking aloud can serve any conceptual or procedural goal and provide us with feedback of how well students are progressing towards these goals.

A great aspect of think-alouds is that they make thinking and progress visible. Growing competence is motivating and creates the continuing impulse to learn (Smith and Wilhelm, 2003). Also, when teaching through think-alouds, we cannot be engaged in information transmission; concepts and procedures are being taught in the purposeful context of inquiry where students are doing the work and learning how to do the work.

I would argue that we want to always be teaching in such a way so that the students are doing the work, and we are helping them to do that work, gradually releasing the responsibility to them. To know how to help, we need to know what they are doing well, where they are struggling, and when and where we can assist them at their current point of need. This is the crucial need formative assessment fulfills.

This is an emphasis that I stress with the pre- and early service teachers with whom I work. The focus must be on students; we have to move from thinking about what *I* am going to today as the teacher to what are *they* going to do today. Creating situations where students do think-alouds, share them, and think about HOW to complete that kind of task is a kind of teaching with your mouth shut where the focus is on students and student activity.

Think-Alouds as Formative Assessment

To a certain extent all formative assessments could be considered a kind of think-aloud because they are ways of making thinking visible and justifying that thinking. This justification of thinking is essential to deep understanding, transfer, and wisdom. Justifying your thinking means telling the story behind the story—considering options and justifying the ones you choose.

Notes-Applications for Writing the Equation of a Line

Becky earns $50 a month plus 3% commission on the selling price on each house she sells.

1. What do you know?

   _____ _____

2. What is the slope?

3. How do we know?

4. What happens if Becky sells no houses?_____

5. Define x = _____ y = _____

6. Slope = _____ Point = _____

7. Write the equation

8. If she sells $500,000 worth of houses, what is her pay?

   x = _____   y = _____

9. Becky wants to earn $4000 next month. What is the cost of the house she needs to sell?

   x = _____   y = _____

Aaron is paid $1200 a month to mow lawns.

10. What do you know? _____

11. Define x = _____ y = _____

12. Write an equation that represents his monthly income?

13. What kind of line is this?

14. What kind of equation do we use?

15. If he works 50 hours in July, what is his pay?

    x = _____   y = _____

Alan earns $8.85 per hour working at Burger Queen.

16. What do you know?

17. What happens if Alan does not work any hours?

18. Define x = _____ y = _____

19. Find Slope: _____ Point: _____

20. Write the equation

21. If he works 12 hours, what is his pay?
    x = _____   y = _____

22. How long does he have to work to earn $327.45.
    x = _____   y = _____

Understanding means that you know HOW you know—you understand your perspective as one among many, and the strategies you use as coming from among repertoires of other alternatives and possibilities. And you know why you have made the choices that you have.

Think-Befores, Think-Durings, Think-Togethers

Think-alouds are typically performed as a kind of thinking *during* the reading or task at hand. But think-alouds can also be very useful prior to undertaking a task to see if you have all the resources and put plans in place. This is the kind of think-aloud Jasmine and I were doing when we planned our way down the whitewater in the introduction to this book. It's a great way to rehearse a task and decompose the elements of the task. Of course, it's very useful to get students to do this kind of think-aloud together.

Think-Afters: Process Analyses as Retrospective Think-Alouds

One purpose served by think-alouds is to get kids to research and monitor their own process of learning—in other words, to learn how to learn and how to improve their own learning process. Getting students to reflect on and make plans for improving their learning processes is essential to this process.

I've been using the process analysis more and more as a retrospective think-aloud to have individual students describe their process of reading, composing, problem-

Process Analysis

A way of reflecting, after the fact (though soon after!) on the process of reading, composing, or solving any problem or navigating any kind of text. The process analysis describes how you went about completing the task, what decisions were made and why, and what options were considered and discarded or could be used in the future. I often use process analyses with the pre- and in-service teachers with whom I work, asking them to compose process analyses of inquiry lessons, classroom activity, peer coaching, or teacher research episodes. The analysis answers these questions:

- What did you do?
- Why did you do it and do it in that order?
- What decisions did you make? Why?
- How did it go? What did you learn?
- What will you do differently next time?

The PA—process analysis—can be composed multimodally with a flow chart, slide show, or other means. Process analyses, also known as reflections, are a requirement of the next generation of assessments, like those associated with the CCSS.

solving, meeting challenging life situations, and so on. I've even begun to have classes share their different PAs and use them to pool their knowledge and come up with a single model analysis for reading a particular kind of text or convention, which becomes a kind of heuristic for efficiently doing the task in the future. (I'm also using this technique extensively with student teachers and the teachers with whom I work in schools to help them reflect on their teaching.)

One of the things that continually surprises both me and my students is that reading, writing, and problem solving of almost any kind is "more complicated" than we originally thought. Naming what we do that works and doesn't work and explaining why brings us all to more "conscious competence"—the goal of all learning and teaching—to understand what we know, how we know it, how we enact it most efficiently, what we can do when things go awry, and so on. A lot of times, we, as readers and human beings, are unconsciously incompetent—we aren't doing things very well, but we are blithely unaware and completely happy. Such an ignorant and happy place to be! Conscious incompetence is when we know something isn't working, but we don't know why or what to do about it. This is a very unhappy place, but better in terms of learning because at least we are aware there is a problem. Sometimes we are unconsciously competent—we are successful but don't know why or how. That means that we can't share what we know, adapt it to new situations, manipulate and extend it, or even replicate our success. What we want for ourselves and for our students is "conscious competence," and process analyses can lead us to this goal.

I don't like to be slavish in what I require for a process analysis, as I want it to work for the learner and this often requires flexibility. I do require that students write about what they were doing—why, what happened (both successes and challenges), choices they made and why, other choices they could make, and what they learned and will do differently next time. Sometimes I offer tips for writing a process analysis, such as the following, but I emphasize that these are just suggestions to guide them.

Before

- What is the task? What are you doing/working on?
- How is it similar to other tasks you've completed in the past? How might this prior experience help you?
- How will the task involve reading and composing?
- How are you feeling about the task?
- How will you get started? What steps will you need to take? How will you divide up the work if this is a group project?
- What is the purpose of the task? How will you know you have been successful?

During

Consider what you are doing, the decisions you are making, options you have, what seems to be working and not working, and why. Talk out loud about it or make some quick notes if you are able so you'll have some reminders afterwards when you compose your process analysis.

After

- What did you do, and in what order?
- Why did you do what you did? And in that order?
- What worked? Why did it work?
- What did not seem to work? Why not? What did you do about this?
- How did you feel at various points in the process?
- What options did you have that you did not play out? What could or will you do differently the next time you have this task or are faced by similar challenges?
- To what degree were you successful? How do you know?
- How can you be even more successful next time?

Process analyses can also be done through drama or visuals. Sometimes students create a flow chart, map, board game, or PowerPoint to express the journey of their learning through a process analysis.

You can expand a process analysis beyond a single assignment or excerpt to describe the learning throughout the inquiry unit itself. Often I've used electronic exit tickets or daily journals that describe think-alouds about the unit, a process analysis of their engagement with the unit itself so far, and so on. On some occasions, I have students write a process analysis paper about their engagement and learning throughout a whole unit.

Three more examples of "think-afters" are stimulated recall, forum drama think alouds, and portfolio cover sheets.

In **stimulated recall,** the teacher typically records students at work completing some kind of task on video or audio. I often use this with student teachers. We then replay the tape of the activity in order to stimulate a commentary upon the participant's thought processes at the time. The participants watch the tape and say what was going on in their head at the time, and why they made the decisions they did, said what they did, and so on. I have also used this technique with visual artifacts students have created, like artwork and video, and ask students to use the artwork as a stimulus to talk about the process of creating it. I also have students create portfolios of work that shows their mastery of course goals and standards, or that show their growth towards these goals, or improvement compared to earlier work and to explain how these goals were addressed.

Forum drama is another way of promoting thinking aloud. In a forum drama an individual or small group can perform a short scenario engaging them in a problem or task. This could be prompted or scripted, mimed or enacted with actions and words. When the performers are done, the audience—or forum—brainstorms: What was she/they thinking? What should she/they be thinking? Why is she/they thinking what she/they are? What is necessary to change her/their thinking? What is she/they thinking now? And now? A variation would be to put a character onto the hotseat and interview them about their thinking throughout the performed scene. If you think the character will lie, mislead, or withhold from you, you can provide another student who will play their inner voice and let the class know what they are really thinking and feeling.

I have students fill out a **portfolio cover sheet** for any work that they think might go in their portfolio. They then choose the best examples for me to consider at the end of the unit or semester. Filling out the form constitutes a kind of think-after. Putting the portfolio together helps them to tell the story of their learning throughout a course of time, and to see and name the ways that they have improved—a salutary and motivating process.

Portfolio Cover Sheet

Title of submitted work sample:

_____

It shows growth in this way . . . when compared to . . .

_____

It shows my progress towards this/these standards and course goals . . . in this way . . .

_____

It shows mastery of this/these standards/goals . . . in this way . . .

_____

Comment from peer on this work sample:

_____

Comment from parent or adult keeper on this work sample:

_____

Teacher comments:

Think-Alouds as Summative Assessment

Think-alouds, particularly in the form of a process analysis accompanying a culminating project or final paper, can be a great complement and contribution to any form of summative assessment.

Remember that teacher research is simply learning from your students how to best teach them. All formative assessments can help you teach the next day's lesson. Summative assessments are less immediately helpful. Rather, they can help you see how well your teaching has fared over the course of a unit when it is complete and consider about what to do differently next time you teach this particular unit and other units and processes (but you better make immediate notes or improvements to your plans and assignment sheets!). In any event, all assessment should aid the development of conscious competence for both student and teacher.

The advantage of think-alouds as an assessment tool is that they give us immediate insight into our students' struggles to formulate and use problem-solving strategies and develop and consolidate insights. Summative assessments can make the process of understanding seem more orderly than it is, covering up the confusion, the disorientation, the mimicry of correct responses, and the lucky guesses, not to mention what students may know and understand but be unable to express on a test or paper, all of which are good to know about when assessing teaching and learning and planning our next phase of instruction.

In the Current

I'm constantly amazed at how fast things move in school, particularly in contrast to my learning outside of school, where I read deeply, take time to reflect and talk to others, and spend time reflecting on, assessing, and then improving my understanding. I'm reminded of Alexander Pope's injunction: "Drink deep or taste not the Pierian spring/a little knowledge is a dangerous thing!"

Sometimes we do indeed read, move, and learn too fast. And sometimes we teach too fast, evaluate too fast, or not at all. Think-alouds are a tool that can slow down reading, and slow down the teaching of reading, so kids get active assistance and contextualized help that can assist them to outgrow their current level of competence to become better readers, writers, and thinkers. Good teaching takes time. If students truly struggle with particular texts and the necessary strategies for comprehending them, then it is up to us as teachers to teach students the strategies they need and to ensure that they get enough practice until they really know and can use the strategy. No one else will do this for the student; it's up to us. The premise behind this whole book is that what is most worth teaching are procedures.

In a world where available information doubles every year, and in which the base of knowledge in a particular subject can dramatically change within a few years, learning how to learn is the most important thing to learn. It's also important to note that the next generation of standards, including the CCSS, are entirely procedural. These new standards do not reward information-driven approaches and will require strategic, inquiry-driven teaching.

With think-alouds in your repertoire, you will teach better, your kids will understand reading better, and you will both be able to name and focus on the text features and interpretive operations required to comprehend them. Students will have the assistance to actually improve their reading performance with all kinds of texts, from the simple to the complex, from narrative to ironic monologue to classifications and argument. You can't get a much better recommendation than that!

Tomorrow, Jasmine and I have a challenge of our own planned. We plan to canoe in the Kenduskeag canoe race. Of course, we went tonight to check out the water flow through all the major drops. We took the time to note the river features and pointed them out to each other, rehearsing what demands each feature would place on us and how we would meet that demand. "Let's make sure to catch that black tongue at Six Mile Falls and eddy out river right in the big eddy there." "Did you see that big hole behind Split Rock! It's a keeper! We'll want to sweep around that to the left!" "If we get caught river left on Shopping Cart Falls, we'll need to eddy out and ferry over to river right." We remind ourselves that one of the ways to self-correct is to backpaddle. By going slower than the current you achieve more control and have more time to make decisions. (This is precisely what think-alouds can do for readers.)

We performed our own think-alouds of our routes and strokes through every rapid. Tomorrow we'll be ready to meet the demands of the river. We'll know if something is going wrong and how to self-correct. We're confident. We're psyched. We feel competent. Okay, I'll admit it, we can't wait!

This is exactly how I want our students to feel when they approach a new and challenging reading task: with knowledge, with confidence, with a desire to successfully complete a slightly more challenging text than they have seen before and to take great pleasure in the text itself, but also with pleasure in being able to name and celebrate their own accomplishment. When they do this they will be readers. They will have moved through many zones of proximal development to the zone we call the reading zone, that place where a reader is totally absorbed in the experience of living through and conversing with the text. And what an adventure that zone can be!

And here's another thing. When we are teaching well and our students are learning, no matter the inevitable struggles, we will be in the "teaching zone," in the "flow" of the most worthy challenge of all human endeavors: that of teaching—of assisting other human beings to outgrow their current selves and grow toward their potential.

Bibliography

Works Cited

Applebee, A. (1993). Literature in the secondary school: Studies of curriculum and instruction in the United States. *NCTE Research Report No. 25*. Urbana, IL: National Council of Teachers of English.

Applebee, A. (1996). *Curriculum as conversation: Transforming traditions of teaching and learning*. Chicago: The University of Chicago Press.

Applebee A. (1998). The teaching of literature in programs with reputations for excellence in English. *Report Series 1.1*. Albany, NY: Center for the Learning and Teaching of Literature.

Baumann, J. (1986). The direct instruction of main idea comprehension ability. In J. F. Baumann (ed.), *Teaching main idea comprehension*, pp. 133–178. Newark, DE: International Reading Association.

Baumann, J. (1992). Teaching comprehension strategies. In B.L. Hayes (ed.), *Effective strategies for teaching reading*, pp. 61–83. Needham Heights, MA: Allyn & Bacon.

Baumann, J., Jones, L. & Seifert-Kessell, N. (1993). Monitoring reading comprehension by thinking aloud. *Instructional Resource Number 1*. Universities of Georgia and Maryland: National Reading Research Center.

Beck, I., McKeown, M., Hamilton, R. & Kugan, L. (1997). *Questioning the Author*. Newark, DE: International Reading Association.

Beck, I. & McKeown, M. (2006). *Improving Comprehension with Questioning the Author*. New York: Scholastic.

Bloom, B. (1976). *Human characteristics and school learning*. New York: McGraw-Hill.

Bloom, B. (Ed.) (1985). *Developing talent in young people*. New York: Ballantine.

Campbell, J., Voelkl, K. & Donahue, P. (1998). NAEP trends in academic progress. Achievement of U.S. students in science, 1969 to 1996; Mathematics, 1973 to 1996; Reading, 1971 to 1996; Writing, 1984 to 1996. Washington D.C.: ED Publications.

Davey, B. (1983). Think aloud—Modeling the cognitive processes of reading comprehension. *Journal of Reading*. v27, n1, pp. 44–47.

Earl, L. (2003). *Assessment as learning: Using classroom assessment to maximize student learning*. Thousand Oaks, CA: Corwin Press.

Edmiston, B. (1991). What have you travelled? A teacher research study of structuring drama for reflection. Unpublished doctoral dissertation, Columbus, OH: The Ohio State University.

Harvey, S. & A. Goudvis. (2007). *Strategies that work*. Portland, ME: Stenhouse.

Heathington, B. (1979). What to do about reading motivation in middle school. *Journal of Reading*, 22, pp. 709–713.

Hillocks, G. (1986). The writer's knowledge: Theory, research, and implications for Practice. In *The teaching of writing: 85th yearbook of the National Society for the Study of Education*, edited by D. Bartholomae and A. Petrosky, pp. 71–94. Chicago: University of Chicago Press.

Hillocks, G. & Smith, M. (1988). Sensible sequencing: Developing knowledge about literature text by text. *English Journal 77* (6): pp. 44–49.

Hillocks, G. (1995). *Teaching writing as reflective practice*. New York: Teachers College Press.

Hillocks, G. (1999). *Ways of thinking, ways of teaching*. New York: Teachers College Press.

McKenna, M., Ellsworth, R. & Kear, D. (1995). Children's attitudes towards reading: A national survey. *Reading Research Quarterly*, 30, pp. 934–957.

National Assessment of Educational Progress. (1981). *Reading, thinking, and writing: Results from the 1979-80 National Assessment of Reading and Literature*. Denver: National Educational Commission of the States.

Newman, F. & Wehlage, G. (1995). *Successful school restructuring: A report to the public and educators by the Center on Organization and Restructuring of Schools.* Madison, WI: Wisconsin Center for Education Research.

Newman, F. & Associates. (1996). *Authentic achievement: Restructuring of schools for intellectual quality,* San Francisco: Jossey-Bass.

Nystrand, M. with Gamoran, A., Kachur, R. & Prendergast, C. (1997). *Opening dialogue: Understanding the dynamics of language and learning in the English classroom.* New York: Teachers College Press.

Pressley, M. & Afflerbach, P. (1995). *Verbal protocols of reading: The nature of constructively responsive reading.* Hillsdale, NJ: Lawrence Erlbaum.

Rabinowitz, P. & Smith, M. (1998). *Authorizing readers: Resistance and respect in the teaching of literature.* New York: Teachers College Press.

Raphael, T. (1982). Question-answering strategies for children. *Reading Teacher* (36)2, pp. 186–190.

Shapiro, J. & White, W. (1991). Reading attitudes and perceptions in traditional and nontraditional reading programs. *Reading Research and Instruction*, 30, pp. 52–66.

Smagorinsky, P. & Smith, M. (1992). The nature of knowledge in composition and literary understanding: A question of specificity. *Review of Educational Research.* 62, pp. 279–306.

Smith, F. (1987). *Joining the Literacy Club: Further essays into education.* Portsmouth, NH: Heinemann.

Smith, M. (1989). Teaching the interpretation of irony in poetry. *Research in the Teaching of English*, 23(3), pp. 254–272.

Smith, M. (1991). *Understanding unreliable narrators.* Urbana, IL: NCTE.

Smith. M. (1998). Teaching argument: A workshop presented to the Maine Writing Project. July 2, 1998.

Smith, M. & Wilhelm, J. (2006). *Going with the flow: How to engage boys (and girls) in their literacy learning.* Portsmouth, NH: Heinemann.

Smith, M. & Wilhelm, J. (2007). *Getting it right.* New York: Scholastic.

Smith, M. & Wilhelm, J. (2002). *Reading don't fix no Chevys: Literacy in the lives of young men.* Portsmouth, NH: Heinemann.

Stauffer, R. (1980). *Directing the reading-thinking process.* New York: Harper and Row.

Taylor, B., Harris, L., Pearson, P. & Garcia, G. (1995). *Reading difficulties, instruction, and assessment (2nd ed.).* New York: McGraw-Hill.

Tharp, R. & Gallimore, R. (1988). *Rousing minds to life: Teaching, learning and schooling in social context.* Cambridge, UK: Cambridge University Press.

Wilhelm, J., Wilhelm, P. & Boas, E. (2009). *Inquiring minds learn to read and write.* Oakville, ONT: Rubicon.

Wilhelm, J. (1997/2008). *You gotta BE the book: Teaching engaged and reflective reading with adolescents.* New York: Teachers College Press.

Wilhelm, J. (2007). *Engaging readers and writers with inquiry.* New York: Scholastic.

Wilhelm, J. (2004). *Reading IS seeing.* New York: Scholastic.

Wilhelm, J. (2002). *Action strategies for deepening comprehension.* New York: Scholastic.

Wilhelm, J., Baker, T. & Dube-Hackett, J. (2001). *Strategic reading.* Portsmouth, NH: Heinemann.

Wilhelm, J. & Edmiston, B. (1998). *Imagining to learn: Inquiry, ethics and integration through drama.* Portsmouth, NH: Heinemann.

Wilhelm, J. & Friedemann, P. (1998). *Hyperlearning: Where projects, inquiry and technology meet.* York, ME: Stenhouse.

Wilhelm, J., Baker, T. & Dube-Hackett, J. (2001). *Strategic reading: Guiding students to lifelong literacy.* Portsmouth, NH: Heinemann/Boynton-Cook.

Index